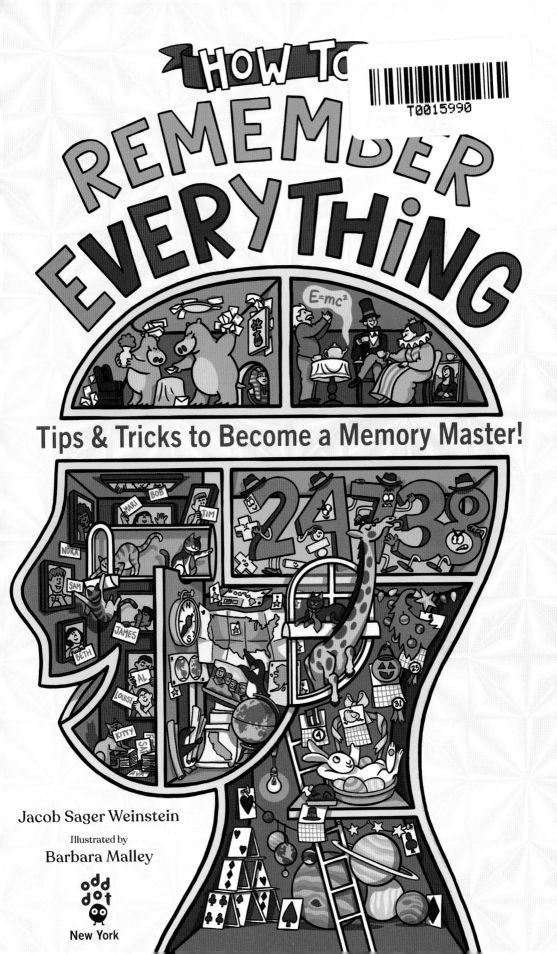

HOW TO REMEMBER EVERYTHING

Tips & Tricks to Become a Memory Master!

Jacob Sager Weinstein

Illustrated by
Barbara Malley

odd dot

New York

For Dennis and Jeanni, with love.
Thanks for letting me store the Seven Wonders
of the Ancient World in your basement
(and for so much else).

Odd Dot is a registered trademark of Macmillan Publishing Group, LLC
120 Broadway, New York, NY 10271 • OddDot.com

Text copyright © 2020 by Jacob Sager Weinstein
Illustrations copyright © 2020 by Barbara Malley

Periodic table on p. 137 © Julie Deshaies/Shutterstock

Library of Congress Cataloging-in-Publication Data
Names: Sager Weinstein, Jacob, author. | Malley, Barbara, illustrator.
Title: How to remember everything / Jacob Sager Weinstein ; illustrated by Barbara Malley.
Description: First edition. | New York : Odd Dot, [2020] | Audience: Ages 10–14 |
Audience: Grades 7–9 | Summary: "Ace history tests by memorizing dates, feel confident
about remembering people's names, kick butt at card games by memorizing entire decks,
and hang on to happy memories for a lifetime. This ultimate memory guide for kids is full of
memory building techniques, fun challenges, and hilarious art" —Provided by publisher.
Identifiers: LCCN 2019043206 (print) | LCCN 2019043207 (ebook) |
ISBN 9781250235268 (paperback) | ISBN 9781250764164 (epub) |
ISBN 9781250764171 (Nook edition)
Subjects: LCSH: Memory—Juvenile literature.
Classification: LCC BF371 .S343 2020 (print) | LCC BF371 (ebook) | DDC 153.1/4—dc23
LC record available at https://lccn.loc.gov/2019043206
LC ebook record available at https://lccn.loc.gov/2019043207

Our books may be purchased in bulk for promotional, educational, or business use. Please
contact your local bookseller or the Macmillan Corporate and Premium Sales Department at
(800) 221-7945 ext. 5442 or by email at MacmillanSpecialMarkets@macmillan.com.

First edition, 2020 • Designed by Carolyn Bahar
Printed in China by 1010 Printing International Limited, North Point, Hong Kong

1 3 5 7 9 10 8 6 4 2

Contents

Introduction:
Me and My Monkeybrain

It was a hot summer day, and adults-only swim seemed to be going on forever. I was seven years old and eager for my chance to cool down. I walked over to the lifeguard and asked him how long it would be until kids were allowed back in the pool.

"About five minutes," he said.

"Thanks," I said.

Now that I had that information, I still had to get back to my mom and my brother, all the way on the other side of the pool. The thought of having to walk across twenty feet of hot concrete crowded any other thoughts out of my mind, and I forgot what the lifeguard had just told me. And so, moments after being told that kids weren't allowed in the pool, I dived in and swam across.

When the lifeguard blew his whistle and yelled at me, I was baffled. What was he so angry about? Fortunately, the puzzled look on my face told him that I wasn't trying to make trouble. I had genuinely forgotten the reason I'd walked over to him in the first place.

That was probably the second-worst memory lapse of my childhood.

The worst was the time I picked up a pen in my right hand and tried to write for several minutes, getting more and more frustrated, before I finally remembered I was left-handed.

What I'm saying is, I'm the most absentminded person I've ever met. Or, at least, the most absentminded person I can *remember* meeting.

And that's why I'm the perfect guy to write a book about memory.

Imagine you want to learn the art of tree-climbing. Which of these animals should you ask for advice?

Naturally tall. Reaches tops of trees without effort. Doesn't understand why you need to climb in the first place. His only advice is, "Be born with a long neck."

Used to fall out of trees when young. Had to pay close attention to how it's done. Can now tell you exactly which branches are safe to bounce on and which ones to avoid.

Well, when it comes to memory, I am a total monkeybrain. As a grown-up, after decades of absentmindedness, I started learning everything I could about how my memory works—and how I could improve it. I read about the ancient secrets that Roman senators used to learn their speeches, and the latest techniques devised by the mental athletes hungry for an edge in the World Memory Championships.

It turns out that many of the greatest **mnemonists** started off as badly as I did. When Dominic O'Brien was ten, for example, his teachers told him he was "terribly slow" and "not going to achieve any success." He went on to be World Memory Champion—eight times!

MNEMONIST
A fancy word for someone who has trained their memory to do amazing things.

As inspired as I was to learn that anybody could improve their memory, I was also a little annoyed. Humanity had discovered many of these techniques thousands of years ago. So how come nobody told me about them sooner? My life would have been completely different.

That's why I wrote this book. I want you to do all the things I couldn't:

- Ace history tests by memorizing dates
- Feel confident about remembering people's names
- Kick butt at card games by memorizing entire decks
- Hang on to happy memories for a lifetime

As with any skill, you'll have to practice. But if you're willing to put in some effort, you'll discover that your mind is capable of amazing feats.

KNEE
2

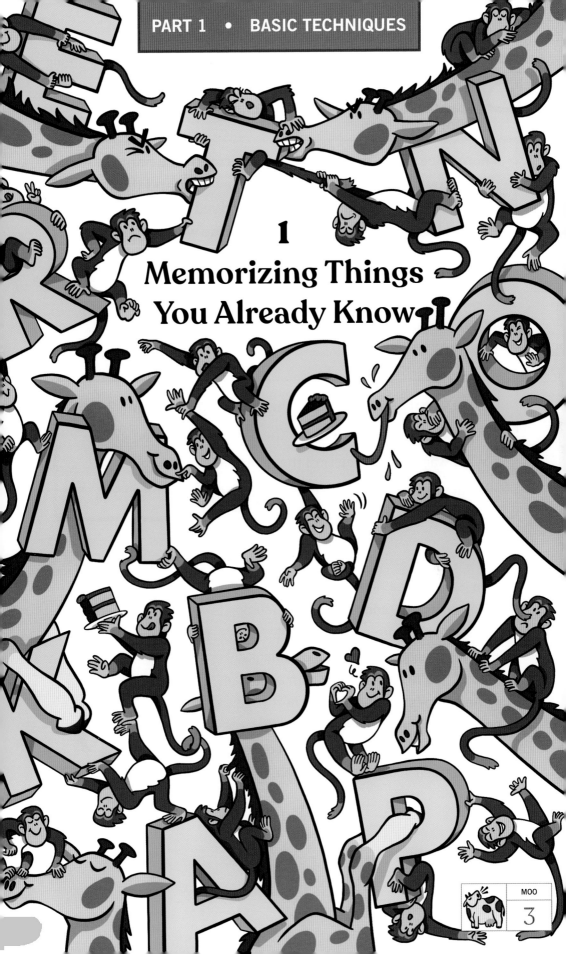

1
Memorizing Things You Already Know

Before we can improve your memory, we have to find out how strong it is in its natural state. Let's put it to a very challenging test. Read the following paragraph once:

> There once was a man. The second letter of the name of his hometown was *o*. He traveled to a new city, and the third letter of that city was *w*. In that city lived a teenager. The second letter of the teenager's last name was *a*. The fourth letter of the grown-up's first name was *c*.

Without looking, did you remember what you read? Let's find out.

> What was the fourth letter of the grown-up's first name?
>
> What was the second letter of the teenager's last name?
>
> What was the third letter of the teenager's home city?
>
> What was the second letter of the grown-up's home city?

If you got all those right after reading the paragraph only once, congratulations! You don't need this book. You are a mental giraffe.

But if you struggled to fill in those blanks, don't worry. You're a completely normal human being. And help is at hand. On the next page, I'm going to tell you a single sentence that is going to let you ace this test. Take a deep breath, and when you're ready, read on.

EAR

4

> Bruce Wayne (who comes from Gotham) battled
> Peter Parker (who comes from New York City).

Okay, cover that last sentence, and let's try another test.

> What was the fourth letter of the grown-up's first name?
>
> What was the second letter of the teenager's last name?
>
> What was the third letter of the teenager's home city?
>
> What was the second letter of the grown-up's home city?

Did you do better? I'm willing to bet you did.

And yet, for the first quiz, you had to memorize only four letters—*C*, *A*, *W*, and *O*. For this one, you had to memorize *B*, *R*, *U*, *C*, *E*, *W*, *A*, *Y*, *N*, *E*, *G*, *O*, *T*, *H*, *A*, *M*, *N*, *E*, *W*, *Y*, *O*, *R*, *K*, *C*, *I*, *T*, *Y*, *P*, *E*, *T*, *E*, *R*, *P*, *A*, *R*, *K*, *E*, and *R*. That's thirty-eight letters! It should have been more than eight times harder!

Of course, you weren't *really* remembering thirty-eight things. You were only remembering one: **Batman fought Spider-Man**.

When you combined those thirty-eight letters into a single idea, you used a classic memory trick. You memorized something by linking it to something you already knew. You had to do some hard work in advance. Before you even opened this book, you had to learn all about Batman's

EEL

5

and Spider-Man's secret identities. But once you did that, you had a context that made memorizing thirty-eight letters a piece of cake.

That's going to be the pattern throughout this book. I'm going to ask you to do some work in advance to master some new skills. Sometimes it may seem like more work than just memorizing things the old-fashioned way! But you'll only have to do that hard work once. And when you have those new skills under your belt, you'll have powerful tools that will make future memorizing easy.

The first skill is one you already use all the time without realizing it. It's called **chunking**. It's what you did when you mashed thirty-eight different letters into a single superheroic image.

CHUNKING

Taking a bunch of different, hard-to-memorize details and combining them into one easy-to-remember chunk.

Chunking

Try chunking the following letters, words, and numbers. Can you come up with a way to reduce each list to a single idea you already know? A * means you can rearrange the list. Otherwise, you have to remember it in the order it's given. I've done the first one to get you started.

1.	*e, m, m, y, o, r
	memory
2.	*snow, little, as, white, its, lamb, had, fleece, was, Mary, a
3.	7, 4, 1, 7, 7, 6
4.	1p = 1000w
5.	1, 0, 1, d
6.	1, 4, 9, 2, c, v

Answer Key

1.	*e, m, y, o, r
	memory
2.	*snow, little, as, white, its, lamb, had, fleece, was, Mary, a
	Mary had a little lamb. Its fleece was white as snow.
3.	7, 4, 1, 7, 7, 6
	7/4/1776 (Independence Day)
4.	1p = 1000w
	A picture is worth a thousand words.
5.	1, 0, 1, d
	101 Dalmatians
6.	1, 4, 9, 2, c, v
	1492: Columbus's voyage

So there you have it. You can memorize ANYTHING, as long as it's something you've already memorized.

That's the end of the book. I hope it was worth what you paid for it. Bye!

What We Learned in CHAPTER 1

1. How to chunk several hard-to-remember things into one memorable idea

2. Whether this book was worth what you paid for it

KEY

7

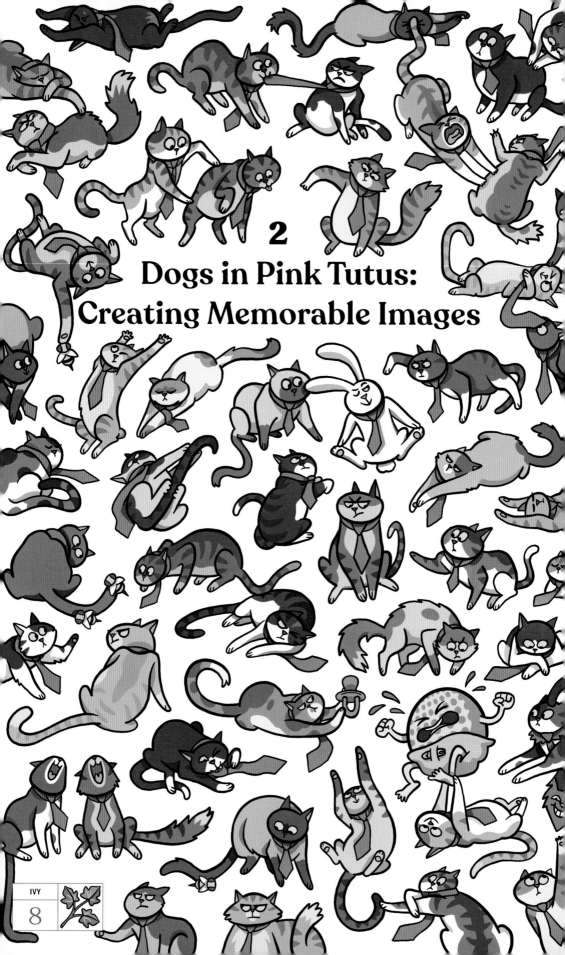

2
Dogs in Pink Tutus: Creating Memorable Images

O kay, that's not *actually* the end of the book. But it's a good introduction to the First Rule of Memory: **The easiest way to remember something is to remember something easy.**

A, a, b, m, n, t is hard to remember. So the First Rule tells us to take the easy way out and to remember "The letters of Batman in alphabetical order" instead.

Unfortunately, the world is full of things that stubbornly refuse to rearrange themselves into the names of superheroes. Fortunately, mnemonists have spent thousands of years coming up with ingenious ways of turning hard things into easy things.

Let's try another experiment. Look at the following pictures:

Now, without looking, describe as many images as you can remember.

I don't know how many you got right, but I'm guessing it wasn't all five.

I'm also guessing there was one you definitely *did* remember: **the tap-dancing dog in a frilly pink tutu**.

That's because bizarre and unusual images are naturally more memorable. You might not have remembered "dog" or "tap-dancing" or "pink" on their own, but when you chunk them—when you squish them together into one silly image—they become much harder to forget. And unlike Batman or Spider-Man, tap-dancing dogs in pink tutus weren't something you'd learned about before you picked up this book (unless you have a very unusual pet).

So it turns out chunking isn't just for things you already know. Chunking can help you remember brand-new things, too.

Imagine that you're a spy. Before you head off on your mission, I hand you a list of password pairs that you have to memorize:

cat	necktie
golf ball	baby
boat	rabbit

If you meet your contact in the moonlit shadow of the Eiffel Tower and he whispers "**cat**," you'll have to whisper back "**necktie**" to prove your identity. On the other hand, if he says "**boat**," you'd better answer "**rabbit**," or he'll disappear into the night.

You might try to learn the pairs just by repeating them over and over again as your spy plane speeds toward Paris. That's how I would have done it before I started studying memory techniques. But now I'd make it easier (and more fun) by imagining a series of ridiculous images.

To remember that "cat" goes with "necktie," **I *could* imagine this.**

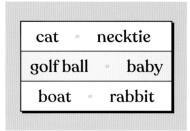

But that wouldn't help me much, because the cat and the necktie aren't interacting at all. It's really

two separate images—one of the cat and one of the necktie. To create a strong mental link, I need to chunk the cat and the necktie together. I need to squish them into a single mental picture.

This one's a little better.

Now the cat and the tie are part of the same image. But it's not very memorable, is it?

So how about this?

That's a little more striking. If you were walking down the street and you saw a cat wearing a necktie, you'd probably remember it for a long time.

But I think we can come up with **an image that is even more vivid and engages our other senses.**

That is the most memorable for me. I can hear the cat yowling in protest, and I can feel him squirming on my chest. And if I take a few extra seconds to imagine the story behind it—if I picture the cat chasing a mouse across my chest and getting tangled up in my tie as he goes—I'm going to have a hard time forgetting it.

You might feel differently. You might think a cat wearing a tie is stranger than a man wearing a cat. For that matter, you might not like that last image because it makes you worry about the cat being hurt. (The cat is fine! He's about to cut himself free with his claws. I'm the one you should be worrying about. I'm allergic to cats!)

TOTE
11

There's no right or wrong answer. Most people find that images become more memorable **when they're strange or shocking, when they use more than one of your senses,** and **when they feel like a story.** But you know better than anybody what you find strange and surprising, what engages your senses, and what kinds of stories make sense to you.

For that matter, you might find that as long as you have a story associated with your image, you don't need to picture it in much sensory detail. Or maybe you'll find that as long as you can smell an image, it doesn't matter how strange it is. Pay attention to your own brain as you use these techniques, and you'll soon figure out which ones work best for you.

And that brings us to the Second Rule of Memory: **Everybody's brain is different.**

Throughout this book, I'll be making big general statements about how memory works. I'll try to make a clear distinction between things that work for me and things that work for most people—but even things that work for most people won't work for everybody. I hope you'll make an effort to try every technique I suggest, but if something doesn't work for you, you are allowed to tweak it until it does—or to skip it entirely.

So one of the following images might work best for you—or even something entirely different.

APHANTASIA

Vivid mental pictures are a crucial part of most memory techniques. But some people can't imagine any images whatsoever. They know that their dog is cute, furry, and brown, but they can't close their eyes and see cute, furry Brownie in their mind.

This is called aphantasia, and as many as one in fifty people might have it.

If you have aphantasia, many memory techniques might not work for you—but some might. Check out verbal mnemonics (chapter 5), the story method (chapter 6), and the Major System (chapter 13). Some aphantasiacs find they can even apply the memory palace system (chapter 4), by using their sense of direction rather than trying to picture a building.

Here's how I might remember the other word pairs:

rabbit • boat

golf ball • baby

waaaaaa!

The Science Behind the Tricks

What makes your brain so powerful isn't the 86 billion neurons inside your skull—it's the 1 quadrillion connections *between* those neurons.

If you just stick something in your brain with no connections . . .

It's going to fall out.

The more details you add, the greater the chance that one of them will connect with something already there.

The more details you add to a new memory, the more connections you make with the neural networks you already have in place.

The technique of adding in elaborate details to make a memory stick has its own elaborate name: **elaboration**. Or at least that's what scientists call it. I prefer to think of it as the Golf Ball in a Diaper technique.

The Science Behind That Last "Science Behind" Section

If I had just said, "Elaboration is a technique for remembering things," the word would have evaporated from your mind a few minutes later. But I gave you more context for it—I explained how it worked, and I tied it into the word "elaborate," which you already knew.

In other words: I used elaboration to help you remember the word "elaboration." Man, I'm good!

Now it's your turn. On the next page, there's a list of word pairs. Come up with an image that unites both words.

Remember to make it as funny or shocking or exciting as you can. To link "**bee**" and "**cannon**," don't just imagine a bee flying near a cannon. Imagine two soldiers trying to fire a cannon *made out of bees.*

Then take a moment to picture it as vividly as you can. Try to involve all your senses—don't just see the image, but hear and smell and feel and maybe even taste it as

well. Hear the soldiers shouting "Ouch" as their bee cannon stings them! Smell the gunpowder drifting across the battlefield! Feel the sticky honey that shoots out every time the bee cannon fires! Taste the sweetness of the glob that lands in your mouth!

Try to work out the story behind the image. How did these soldiers end up bringing a bee cannon into battle?

Of course, when your assignment is "make a silly image," there's no right or wrong answer. These images could be just as memorable:

bee	cannon
truck	branch
note	hook
oranges	shave
blink	home
crown	bounce
wrist	cracker
pipe	lunchroom
hat	moon
jellyfish	marble

If you've been following my instructions literally, you haven't actually tried to memorize the pairs I gave you—you've just been imagining memorable links between them. But I bet in the process, you actually *have* memorized the pairs.

Cover up the second word in every pair and see if you remember it.

How'd you do? If you got seven or more, congratulations! You're on your way to becoming a master mnemonist.

And if not, don't worry. Go back and review the connections you came up with. Are they as strange, funny, or shocking as you can make them? Imagine them as vividly as you can, using all your senses. Then give it another try.

True Tales of Jacob's Monkeybrain

Every night before I went to bed, my parents would ask me if I brushed my teeth. I always said yes. I wasn't lying—I had a definite memory of doing it at some point. I couldn't be sure if I was remembering something from that evening or from two days ago, but I always gave myself the benefit of the doubt.

I probably shouldn't have. I ended up having to get four fillings by the time I went off to college.

Sadly for me and my teeth, I didn't know the Golf Ball in a Diaper method of making memorable images—but you do, and you can use it to ward off cavities. As you're brushing your teeth at night, think about something you did during the day that you don't do every day. Come up with an image to represent it—and then stick a toothbrush into it.

If you visited your grandmother's house, picture her battling an angry foaming toothbrush. If you played field hockey, imagine everybody using giant toothbrushes to swat the ball.

When you try to remember if you brushed your teeth, that image will pop into your head, and you'll know you did it *today*, not three days ago.

You can use this technique for any task you have to do regularly, like taking out the trash or walking the dog.

TICK

17

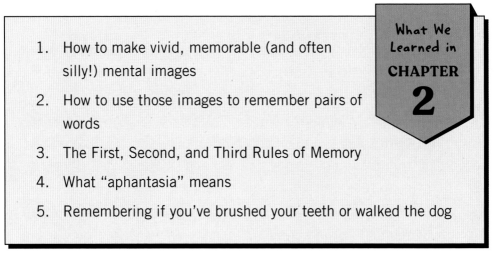

What We Learned in **CHAPTER 2**

1. How to make vivid, memorable (and often silly!) mental images

2. How to use those images to remember pairs of words

3. The First, Second, and Third Rules of Memory

4. What "aphantasia" means

5. Remembering if you've brushed your teeth or walked the dog

ANSWER KEY | FAKE ITEM: 3 (WE HAVEN'T LEARNED THE THIRD RULE OF MEMORY YET.)

TAFFY

18

3
Miss-a-Sippy-Cup:
Remembering
Abstract Things

TAPE
19

I f you're starting to get the hang of it, let's try something harder. Some of the pairs on this page will require you to remember longer phrases. For longer phrases, it's sometimes helpful to think about an action instead of just an image.

To link **"maid's son"** with **"whisk,"** I might **picture something like this.**

Other pairs (like **"August, mane"**) require you to imagine more abstract words. To picture "August," you might think about the things you associate with it, like hot summer days. **I might imagine something like this.**

Now it's your turn! Try to come up with the craziest and most vivid images you can to link each of these pairs. Then cover up one item in each pair and see if you can remember it.

maid's son	whisk
August	mane
little rock	ark
to peek	the Wizard of Oz
spring in a field	ill and annoyed
den	colors
phoenix	arise
jack-in-the-box's son	sippy cup
Christopher Columbus	high
Atlantis	George

That was harder, wasn't it? If you got fewer than seven right, don't worry! Just go back and make those images even more memorable. Make them sillier or more surprising, and really take the time to use all your senses.

For "**colors**," don't just picture blue or red—picture an entire rainbow arcing across the sky. Now imagine you've come to the end of the rainbow, but instead of gold, there's a bear's den. Colors drip from the rainbow onto the bear's fur. Hear him growling as you hunt through his den and find a rainbow-colored pot of gold. Feel your fear as he chases you right out of his den!

If you got seven or more right, congratulations! You're going to make a great spy. But if you don't have a secret mission to Paris today, you can use this technique for other things, too.

For example, suppose you want to memorize the state capitals. Here's a list of ten of them:

Madison, Wisconsin
Augusta, Maine
Little Rock, Arkansas
Topeka, Kansas
Springfield, Illinois
Denver, Colorado
Phoenix, Arizona
Jackson, Mississippi
Columbus, Ohio
Atlanta, Georgia

Some of those places are easy to turn into an image. For "**Little Rock**," we can just imagine a little rock.

For others, we'll need to be a bit creative. The word "**Madison**" looks like "**maid's son**," so that's what we'll picture. **Kansas** is where Dorothy lives before the tornado sends her off on her adventure, so we'll picture the **Wizard of Oz**. And for **Mississippi**, we'll make a pun and think of it as "**Miss-a-sippy-cup**."

Wait a minute. Maid's son . . . the Wizard of Oz . . . sippy cup . . . those are all words from the last set of pairs you just memorized. While you were learning your spy passwords, those pairs were on a secret mission of their own: smuggling state capitals into your brain. That's because *all* those pairs were disguised states and their disguised capitals.

Now YOU Try It!

State Capitals

Can you figure out which word pair is really a disguised version of which state and capital pair?

Springfield, Illinois	little rock · ark
Topeka, Kansas	Atlantis · George
Jackson, Mississippi	to peek · The Wizard of Oz
Augusta, Maine	maid's son · whisk
Little Rock, Arkansas	phoenix · arise
Columbus, Ohio	Christopher Columbus · high
Atlanta, Georgia	August · mane
Denver, Colorado	jack-in-the-box's son · sippy cup
Madison, Wisconsin	spring in a field · ill and annoyed
Phoenix, Arizona	den · colors

Answer Key

Phoenix, Arizona	=	phoenix • arise
Madison, Wisconsin	=	maid's son • whisk
Denver, Colorado	=	den • colors
Atlanta, Georgia	=	Atlantis • George
Columbus, Ohio	=	Christopher Columbus • high
Little Rock, Arkansas	=	little rock • ark
Augusta, Maine	=	August • mane
Jackson, Mississippi	=	jack-in-the-box's son • sippy cup
Topeka, Kansas	=	to peek • the Wizard of Oz
Springfield, Illinois	=	spring in a field • ill and annoyed

Go over that list and imagine those crazy pairs one more time. Make sure you understand how each state or capital is transformed into a memorable word. Can you see how "**arise**" is hidden inside "**Arizona**"? Can you hear how "**Illinois**" sounds like "**ill and annoyed**"?

When you're done picturing those images, cover the capitals in the list below and see how many you can remember.

Georgia	Atlanta
Colorado	Denver
Mississippi	Jackson
Maine	Augusta
Wisconsin	Madison
Kansas	Topeka
Arizona	Phoenix
Ohio	Columbus
Illinois	Springfield
Arkansas	Little Rock

If you got fewer than seven right, don't worry! Practice will make perfect.

If you got seven or more correct, congratulations! You've mastered some of the most important techniques in memory training. Plus, you're on your way to learning all the state capitals.

Once you know how to make crazy mental mashups to link words and phrases, you can remember all sorts of things.

GNOME

23

Now YOU Try It!

Useful Distinctions

If we want to remember the difference between an alligator and a crocodile, we should NOT chunk an alligator and a crocodile together. That would only make things more confusing! Instead, we should chunk an alligator with an alligator fact, and then come up with a separate image that chunks a crocodile with a crocodile fact.

Alligators have a shovel-shaped jaw.

Crocodiles have pointed jaws, like an arrowhead or the letter *V*.

Penguins live in the Antarctic.

Polar bears live in the Arctic.

All our examples so far have linked one thing to another—a state to its capital, or penguins to the Antarctic. But sometimes you'll want to link one thing to dozens or even thousands of other things. For example, if you're learning French, you'll need to memorize which nouns are masculine and which ones are feminine. Before you sit down with a vocabulary list, come up with a **standard modification**.

STANDARD MODIFICATION

A way of tweaking an image to help you remember a common, repeated fact.

If you're studying French vocabulary, for example, you might picture every **f**eminine noun as **f**reezing, and every **m**asculine noun as **m**elting.

la souris
a freezing mouse

le chat
a melting cat

Pay Attention!

From now on, the review at the end of every chapter may include **entries with questions**. When you get to one, stop and test your memory by trying to answer it. But watch out! There's still going to be a **fake fact** in every review.

1. How to transform vague words (like "color")
   into concrete images (like a rainbow)

2. How to picture scenes to remember phrases
   like "a maid's son"

3. How to use puns and sound-alikes to
   remember tricky words like "Mississippi"

4. Albert Einstein's personal memory technique

5. The capitals of ten states

6. The difference between alligators and crocodiles (What is it?)

7. Where polar bears live, and where penguins live (Where do
   they live?)

8. What a standard modification is

ANSWER KEY | FAKE ITEM: 4

Now YOU Try It!

Planets and Their Moons

After every chapter, I'll give you the chance to use
the technique you've just learned to memorize
something new.

Memorize which planet each of the following moons orbits.

Luna	○	Earth
Deimos	○	Mars
Ganymede	○	Jupiter
Titan	○	Saturn
Titania	○	Uranus
Triton	○	Neptune

Then cover the planets with your hand and test your recall.

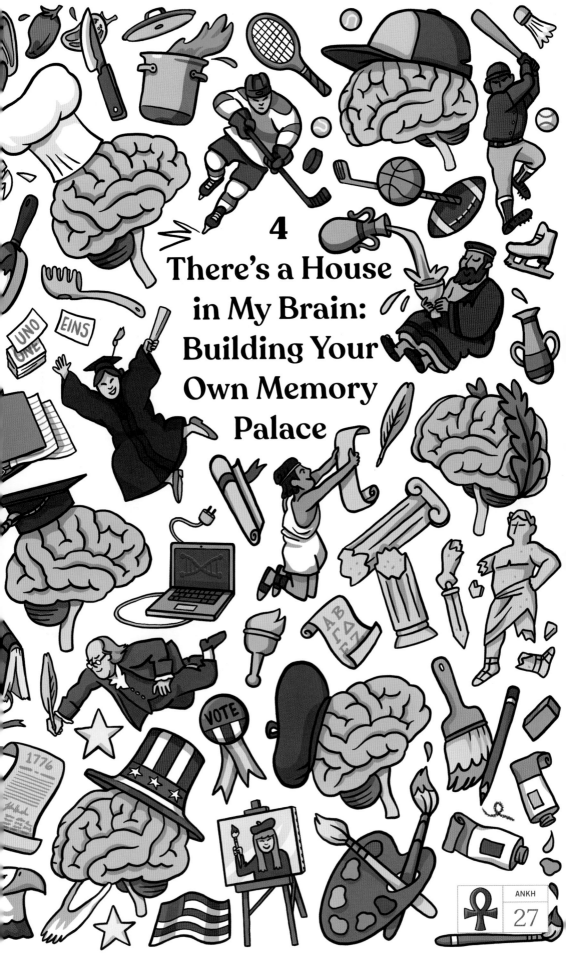

4

There's a House in My Brain: Building Your Own Memory Palace

Twenty-five hundred years ago, a rich Greek nobleman threw a party. His favorite boxer had just won a big match, and when your favorite boxer wins, there's only one thing to do: eat, drink, and commission a victory ode.

So the rich man summoned a famous poet, promising him plenty of drachmas if he'd write something for the occasion. Because he knew who was paying the bill, the poet made sure to write about how great the rich man was. And because he was a good ancient Greek, he made sure to praise the gods, too—especially Pollux (who was renowned as a boxer) and his twin brother, Castor.

The poet had kept his part of the deal, but it turned out the rich man wasn't as honest. With the poem safely in hand, he announced he was cutting the poet's fee in half. "If you love Castor and Pollux so much, let them pay the rest," snickered the rich man.

At that moment, a messenger rushed in to tell the poet there were two young men waiting outside for him. He went out to meet them—but they had vanished.

He turned to go back inside the rich man's palace. Before he took another step, the entire building collapsed, killing everybody inside. The two disappearing young men had been Castor and Pollux themselves, and by summoning the poet, they had saved his life.

As the only survivor, the poet had the grim task of identifying the smooshed bodies. There were dozens of people at the feast, but he found he could remember every single one, just by picturing the spot where they had been sitting.

KNIFE

28

The poet's name was Simonides. And from his strange adventure, he drew two conclusions:

　　1. Never mock the gods when you're sitting under something heavy.

　　2. It's easier to remember things when you can picture where they are.

Simonides could have used this experience to found any number of disciplines. He could have become the Father of Building Safety, or the Father of Always Getting Paid in Advance. Instead, he became the Father of Memory, credited with inventing one of the most important techniques in the mnemonic arts.

People who like fancy Greek names call it the **method of loci**. ("Loci" just means "places" in Greek.) Others call it the **memory palace**, or the **memory walk**. Whatever name it goes by, it's extremely powerful. Let's take it for a stroll, shall we?

Study this list of fifteen words. When you think you've got them memorized, cover them up and try to recite them in order.

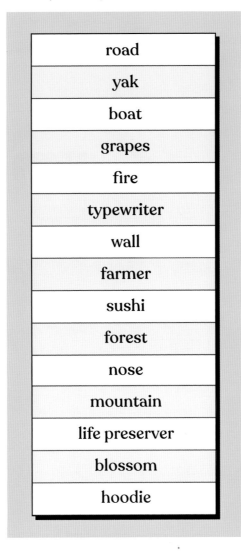

road
yak
boat
grapes
fire
typewriter
wall
farmer
sushi
forest
nose
mountain
life preserver
blossom
hoodie

How'd you do? If you just tried reciting the list to yourself, you probably got five to nine words—that's the number most people can hold in their short-term memory.

After reading the last chapter, you know that making vivid images helps you link words together. Maybe you had the clever idea of linking each item to the next—of picturing a yak with a road in his fur, and then a boat piloted by yaks, and so on. If you came up with this technique on your own, congratulations! You've independently invented another classic memory technique— and you didn't even need the help of the gods to do it.

It's an excellent technique, and it can be useful in many circumstances. But it has one weakness: if you forget one item, you can lose the entire chain.

So let's try something else. Once again, we'll link the words to something we already know. And as Simonides recognized, there's little we know better than the places we've been.

Imagine the place you know best— whether it's your home, or your favorite store, or a local park. Pick a starting place for a walk around. For example, if you've chosen your home, you might start at your **bed**.

The first word we have to memorize is **road**. Imagine that your bedsheets have a picture of a road on them—and that, magically, the road turns real, stretching off your bed and running into the distance.

In your room, you probably have a bedside table. Picture a big, hairy **yak** grazing on your alarm clock. (Smell him, too, if you dare.)

A logical next place to go would be your bureau to get your clothes. Only this time, when you pull open a drawer, there's a miniature lake inside it, with a **boat** floating on it.

Now walk out of your bedroom, taking a moment to pluck the **grapes** hanging from the doorframe. Instead of family photos, there's a giant **nose** growing out of the wall in the hallway. Also, instead of a carpet, there's a massive **fire**, so run quickly down the **typewriter** that has replaced the staircase, hearing that distinctive *clickety-clack* sound as your feet hit the keys.

You know your house better than I do. Maybe that staircase leads to the kitchen, or maybe it leads to the private basketball court in which you, the NBA's top-scoring player, relentlessly practice your three-point shots. (Hey, I never know who's going to be reading my books.) Whatever the case may be, keep walking on a logical path through this real place, stocking it with outrageous images from the word list as you go.

When you're done, cover up the words again. Imagine yourself back at your starting point, and try once more to recall the word list.

I'm guessing you did much better. In fact, I'd bet my house on it!

MAT
HELLO

The Science Behind the Technique

The human brain didn't evolve to memorize shopping lists and American presidents—it evolved to keep us alive as we hunted and gathered. If your distant ancestors couldn't remember where the berries grew in the African wilds, they would starve. If they couldn't remember the safe path through the snake-filled marsh, they'd drown. To this day, our brains are good at remembering where things are.

And if they saw something shocking (like a tiger bursting through an improperly built wall), they would need to remember it so they could stop it from happening again. As a result, our brains are also good at remembering crazy and unusual images.

As the First Rule of Memory suggests, most memory techniques are just sneaky ways of converting stuff our brain isn't good at remembering into things it *is* good at. You're tricking yourself into storing stuff in an entirely different part of your brain. Indeed, if you put a master mnemonist inside an MRI or other brain-scanning machine, you can see the regions of the brain that usually handle images and locations lighting up as they memorize numbers and words.

In our example, we didn't cram too many images into each room. In your bedroom, for instance, we stored one thing in your bed, one thing grazing on your alarm clock, and something else in your bureau. Then we headed out the door. Now that you've got the hang of it, I bet you can find a lot more places to tuck images away.

It will take some practice to figure out how many locations you can get out of each room before you lose track of the order to visit them in, or forget about some of them entirely. One tip: try not to have too many similar locations. Your real-life bookshelf may have dozens of shelves, but your memory palace should just use your bookshelf to store one single thing. Otherwise, you might run into **interference**.

INTERFERENCE

When two memories are similar (or related in some other way), they can get mixed up. This is called interference. You've experienced it if you've ever said a wrong word that sounds like the right one, or searched in the pockets of your light-blue coat for something you actually left in your light-blue jeans.

True Tales of Jacob's Monkeybrain

My wife's name is Lauren. My daughter's name is Erin. Maybe they sound totally different to you, but thanks to interference, my brain is constantly pulling the wrong name off its List of Beloved Females Whose Names End in *N*.

My son's name is Joseph, which (like Jacob) is a Biblical Name Starting with *J*. But even I'm not so absentminded that I'd confuse myself with my own son. Now if you'll excuse me, I've got to hurry off to fifth grade.

Memory Walk Puzzle

Memory palaces are especially useful for any list with an order. Can you figure out what this memory walk represents?

Answer Key

James, man! Row!

JAMES MONROE

I'm mad at you, son!

JAMES MADISON

In 2017, twelve-year-old Mrunali Gouri Kodhe of India set a new world record for the Most Objects Memorized in One Minute. She had sixty seconds to examine a table with fifty-three objects. Then the judges mixed up the objects, and she had fifteen minutes to put them back in the correct order. She got fifty of them right, beating out the previous record of forty-five.

Memory palaces aren't just for ordered lists. They can also prevent interference, by making similar things seem more different. If you're studying botany, for example, you might need to know the Latin names of a ton of plants. If you put each one in a separate mental room, you're less likely to confuse your *Morus rubra* with your *Morus alba*.

Morus rubra

You can also use this technique to remember directions. Let a memory walk guide you on an actual walk! Come up with crazy images for each street name, and use a standard modification to remember the direction. I'm left-handed, so I always picture left-hand turns as happy and right-hand turns as sad.

Morus alba

If you've used a memory palace to store something you don't need permanently, you can always reuse it to store

something new. Some people find it helpful to do a mental walkthrough, deleting each item, and reimagining the location as it actually is.[1]

But if you *do* want to remember something permanently, you're better off dedicating a memory palace to only that topic. Otherwise, you'll run into interference.

Turn right on
Pine Street.

1. Personally, I don't find that necessary. That's the advantage of being so absentminded—my memory palaces fade naturally if I don't make the effort to review them!

The second president of the United States was um . . . John Boatyflood?

That means you're going to need a lot of memory palaces! Fortunately, you aren't limited to real-life buildings you've visited. If you can picture the place vividly, and it has distinct locations within it, you can use it to store memories. That might include:

- **Fictional locations** from your favorite books and movies.
- **Imaginary places** that you created yourself, whether in your mind, on paper, or with Legos.
- **Video game levels**. You could even build your own memory palace in Minecraft.
- **Real-life places** you've studied through photographs or an online virtual tour. You don't have to be a pharaoh to store things in the Great Pyramids.
- **Parts of your body**. Writing down the answers on the back of your hand is cheating. *Imagining* you've written them there is just studying!

Welcome to wizard school, Harry!

Now YOU Try It!

Presidential Challenge

The images I use for the presidents might not be the same as the ones you would use. Come up with your own. And while you're at it, why not memorize the first *ten* presidents?

1.	George Washington
2.	John Adams
3.	Thomas Jefferson
4.	James Madison
5.	James Monroe
6.	John Quincy Adams
7.	Andrew Jackson
8.	Martin Van Buren
9.	William Henry Harrison
10.	John Tyler

Now cover the box above with your hand.
Who were the first ten presidents?

What We Learned in CHAPTER 4

1. The mythical origins of the memory palace
2. How the ancient Greeks elected their leaders
3. How to use a memory palace to store ordered lists
4. The first ten American presidents
5. The kinds of places you can use for memory palaces

ANSWER KEY | FAKE ITEM: 2

The Continents, from Smallest to Largest

Memorize the seven continents from smallest to largest.

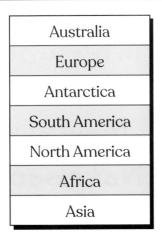

Australia
Europe
Antarctica
South America
North America
Africa
Asia

Now cover the box above with your hand.
What are the seven continents, from smallest to largest?

MAP
39

Interlude:
Your
Memory
Notebook

It's time to get out a notebook—a real one on your desk, or a virtual one on your phone or computer—and start writing things down.

I know what you're saying: *Jacob, you're supposed to be teaching me how to memorize stuff. Isn't writing things down cheating?*[2]

No! A notebook can serve a number of useful purposes. You can use it to organize facts before you store them, and to write down things you want to memorize but haven't yet. And as we'll see in chapter 10, even the best-trained memory needs regular review to lock things in permanently.

---

2. Unless you're saying, "Help me, Jacob! I'm being chased by wolves!" In that case, keep running until you reach a bookshop, and buy a copy of my book <u>How to Avoid Getting Chased by Anything.</u>

Start your notebook with two lists. (If you're using a real notebook, leave plenty of space between them so you can add to them later.)

1. Things I Want to Memorize

2. Places I Know Well Enough to Use as Memory Palaces

There might be some things on that first list that you don't yet know how to memorize. *(How do I store people's phone numbers in a memory palace? Am I supposed to imagine each digit, using all my senses? How the heck does a seven smell?)* Don't worry—there are still twelve chapters to come. By the end of the book, you'll be able to memorize numbers as easily as state capitals.

If one of the things you want to memorize is suitable for a memory walk, then go ahead and choose a palace to store it in. If one of the locations seems like a natural fit, that's great. By all means, store that list of French royalty in the halls of Versailles. But don't get too hung up on thematic unity.

It's more important to pick a palace that's got the right number of locations. That tiny tent where you once camped in the middle of the desert may not be the best place to cram in all 118 elements on the periodic table. And if you can picture every square inch of the Empire State Building, you may not want to waste it on memorizing the names of the four Beatles.

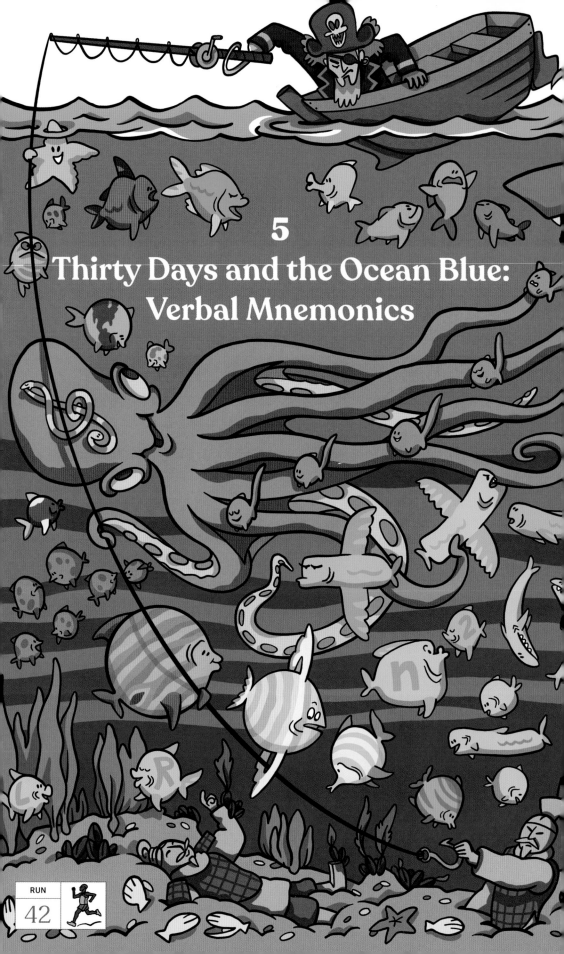

5

Thirty Days and the Ocean Blue:
Verbal Mnemonics

The techniques we've used are great for things that are easy to visualize, like lists of objects. You've probably noticed that they take more work when you're memorizing something more abstract, like "Wisconsin." And sometimes, it's just too much work to come up with a picture for something.

Suppose you're always misspelling "calendar" as "calender." You *could* try to come up with a vivid image for every letter, then put them in order along a memory walk. But if you want to remember a bunch of words permanently, you're going to use up an awful lot of memory palaces. Plus, it's a lot of unnecessary work.

There's only one letter in the word that you get wrong, but you're coming up with eight images for it.

For a situation like that, it's helpful to have another tool in your arsenal: the **verbal mnemonic**.

You probably know a bunch of these already:

I wish I could remember why I put that <u>M</u> at the beginning of my name.

MNEMONIC

A mnemonic is any trick for remembering things. The word comes from Mnemosyne, the Greek goddess of memory.

A visual mnemonic is one that uses pictures. We talked about those in the previous chapters.

A verbal mnemonic is one that uses words.

In 1400 and 92,
Columbus sailed the ocean blue.

Thirty days hath September,
April, June, and November.

The angry pirate shouted, "Arr!
Make sure you spell it calen-**dar**!"

CALEN-DAR!

Okay, you probably don't know that last one, because I just made it up. It's not the greatest poem ever written—but neither are the other two. Verbal mnemonics don't have to be great art. They just have to stick in your brain.

Rhymes help, but they aren't always necessary. When I kept forgetting that the person in charge of a school was a "principal" instead of a "principle," my mom told me, "The princi**pal** is your **pal**." Decades later, I still think of that whenever I write the word.

Verbal mnemonics become even catchier when they're sung. You probably learned the alphabet by singing it. And you can learn the dynasties of China by singing to the tune of "Frère Jacques":

Shang, Zhou, Qin, Han
Shang, Zhou, Qin, Han
Sui, Tang, Song
Sui, Tang, Song
Yuan, Ming, Qing, Republic
Yuan, Ming, Qing, Republic
Mao Zedong
Mao Zedong

As I was writing this book, my editor, Daniel, told me that he learned the quadratic equation to the tune of "Pop Goes the Weasel":

x equals negative b
plus or minus the square root
of b-squared minus 4ac,
all over 2a

I wish I had learned it that way. In fact, I wish I had learned *everything* set to music.

Sometimes a mnemonic can be as simple as an intentional mispronunciation. I can't spell "definitely" without mumbling "de-FINITE-ly" to myself.

Some verbal mnemonics help you remember a bunch of words at once:

I before E,
except after C,
or when sounded like A
as in "neighbor" and "weigh."

And to remember just a few of the many exceptions to that rhyme, there's the crazy sentence "Neither feisty leisured foreigner seized their weird beige height, Weinstein."

Here are some commonly misspelled words. I've suggested mnemonics for the first few. But as with visual mnemonics, the best verbal mnemonics are the ones you come up with yourself. Can you come up with the rest?

Word	Misspelling	Mnemonic
basically finally incidentally	basicly finaly incidently	Fin**ally** in trouble? Basic**ally**, incident**ally** is your **ally**.
Caribbean	Carribean	When you sail Caribbean seas, Bring one *R*, but bring two *B*s.
cemetery	cemetary	Everyone yells EEE! when they pass a cemetery.
persistent	persistant	
separate	seperate	
tomorrow	tomorow tommorow	

Verbal mnemonics aren't just for spelling. Every time I tighten or loosen a screw, I think, "Righty tighty, lefty loosey."

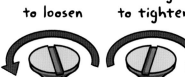

Turn left to loosen   Turn right to tighten

Another type of verbal mnemonic uses the first letter of each word as an **acronym** to hint at what you're supposed to remember.

ACRONYM

An acronym is an abbreviation formed from the first letters of the words in a phrase. Some acronyms have become so common that people are surprised to learn what they stand for. Believe it or not, the words "laser" and "radar" are both acronyms: **L**ight **A**mplification by **S**timulated **E**mission of **R**adiation, and **RA**dio **D**etection **A**nd **R**anging.

A mnemonic can even be a pretend acronym. When my kids struggled with the spelling of "would," I taught them to imagine it stood for "Would Old Underpants Lie Down?"

Here are a few acronym mnemonics you might already know:

Order of the Planets from the Sun:

My **V**ery **E**ducated **M**other **J**ust **S**erved **U**s **N**oodles
(Mercury, Venus, Earth, Mars, Jupiter, Saturn, Uranus, Neptune)

Notes on a Treble Clef:

Every **G**ood **B**oy **D**eserves **F**udge

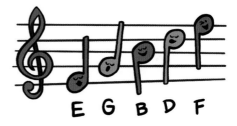

Order in Which You Do Mathematical Operations:

Please **E**xcuse **M**y **D**ear **A**unt **S**ally
(Parenthesis, Exponents, Multiplication, Division, Addition, Subtraction)

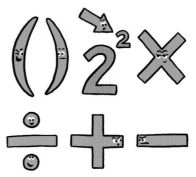

Order of the Colors of the Rainbow:

Sometimes we just take the first letter of each word and don't bother with a new sentence. You might know the colors of the rainbow as ROY G BIV (**R**ed, **O**range, **Y**ellow, **G**reen, **B**lue, **I**ndigo, **V**iolet).

RAKE
47

Memorizing Poems

A lot of verbal mnemonics are short poems. But what if the thing you need to remember *is* a poem?

If it's short enough, you probably don't need any mnemonic techniques at all. The poem will act as its own mnemonic!

But for longer poems, you might need some help:

- Break it down into a series of small enough units that you can memorize them easily.
- Use any of the techniques in this book to remember the order of the units. Some examples:
  - You could make an acronym from the first letter of every line.
  - You can assign one or more images to every couplet and store them in a memory palace.
  - Sometimes you can find a tune that fits the poem. Many poems and songs are written in a meter so common that it's come to be known as—you guessed it—the common meter. As a result, you can sing "Because I could not stop for Death" and *The Rime of the Ancient Mariner* to any one of dozens of songs, including the *Pokémon* theme song and "Amazing Grace." Even poems not in the common meter may have a song equivalent.

In chapters 8 and 13, I'll teach you how to turn numbers into concrete, easy-to-remember images. But until you get the hang of that, you can use another kind of verbal mnemonic. If you want to recall a certain famous mathematical constant, just say "Mom, I want a giant chocolate to nibble daily." The number of letters in each word tells you the next digit of pi.

3 1 4 1 5   9 2 6 5

Mom, I want a giant chocolate to nibble daily.

I'll be honest: most of the time, visual mnemonics stick better in my head. I mainly find verbal mnemonics useful for things that don't make vivid pictures (like individual letters or abstract concepts). But as the Second Rule of Memory says, *Everybody's brain is different*. If you find yourself struggling to get a picture of something into your memory, it's always worth trying one of the verbal techniques in your mnemonic arsenal.

You might even bust out a two-step process: first, come up with a verbal mnemonic, and second, use a crazy picture to lodge it firmly in your brain.

Now YOU Try It!

Mnemonic Quiz
Every one of these images is a mnemonic we've covered in this chapter. Can you figure out what they are?

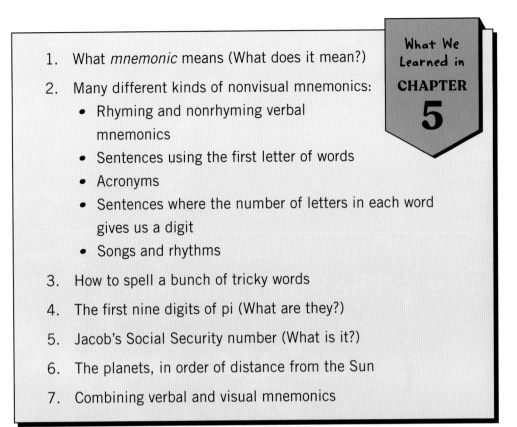

1. What *mnemonic* means (What does it mean?)
2. Many different kinds of nonvisual mnemonics:
   - Rhyming and nonrhyming verbal mnemonics
   - Sentences using the first letter of words
   - Acronyms
   - Sentences where the number of letters in each word gives us a digit
   - Songs and rhythms
3. How to spell a bunch of tricky words
4. The first nine digits of pi (What are they?)
5. Jacob's Social Security number (What is it?)
6. The planets, in order of distance from the Sun
7. Combining verbal and visual mnemonics

What We Learned in CHAPTER 5

ANSWER KEY | FAKE ITEM: 5

Now YOU Try It!

The Speed of Light

The speed of light is 299,792,458 meters per second. You can remember that with the following verbal mnemonic, in which the number of letters in each word tells you the next digit:

My universal racetrack limited refueling, so UFOs crash suddenly.

Now cover the box above with your hand.
What is the speed of light?

6
Once Upon a Time:
The Story Method

Pop quiz! Not too long ago, I told you a story about a rich man and a poet named Simonides. Try to answer these questions without turning back to check:

In what country did the rich man and the poet live?
What was the rich man celebrating?
What did he hire the poet to do?
How did he treat the poet?
How did the rich man die?
Why did the poet survive?
What grisly job did the poet have to do after the tragedy?

You didn't try to memorize any of those details, but I bet you got a bunch of them right. That's because stories—like places—naturally stick in the human mind. And that gives us another trick we can use to remember stuff: the story method.

Let's say you want to remember the order of the planets, but you don't like the verbal mnemonic from the last chapter. You might tell yourself the following story:

> Because the **mercury** was so high in the thermometer, **Venus** Williams decide to leave **Earth**. She blasted off to **Mars**. "Jumping **Jupiter**," she yelled. "I just **sat on** a pin. I hate you, pin. You're a **nuisance**." Tired from the trip, she put on her **nap tunes** and went to sleep.

In many ways, the story method is halfway between a verbal mnemonic and a memory walk. It has the strengths of both methods. Like a verbal mnemonic, it can be useful for words you find hard to visualize. Like a memory walk, it can help you keep things in order.

LLAMA
53

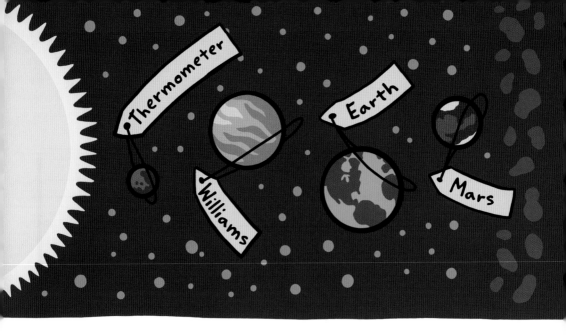

On the other hand, it has the weaknesses of both, too. Like with a verbal mnemonic, you have to make up a new one for everything you want to remember. And like a memory walk, you can find yourself unsure of how to translate a story back to the original items.

So what's the best mnemonic technique to use—the one that's perfect for every circumstance?

There isn't one, any more than there's one pitch that's right to throw against every batter. With time, though, you'll get a feel for which techniques work best for you.

What We Learned in

CHAPTER

6

1. The story method

2. When Venus Williams won her first championship

3. The order of planets in the distance from the Sun (if you didn't learn it in the last chapter)

ANSWER KEY | FAKE ITEM: 2

Now YOU Try It!

The Longest Rivers
Here are the five longest rivers in the world. Come up with a story to help you remember them.

Nile
Amazon
Yangtze
Mississippi
Yenisei

Now cover the box above with your hand.
What are the five longest rivers in the world?

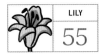

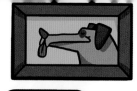

7

Is That a Rose on Your Head?
Remembering People's Names

LOG
56

True Tales of Jacob's Monkeybrain

People with good memories can confidently extend their hands to folks they don't recognize and say, "Nice to meet you." Me? I say, "Nice to *see* you," just in case I've met them before. And when somebody introduces me to their friend with, "Jacob, have you met John?" I dodge the question with a cheerful, "How are you, John?"

Once, when I was a teenager, I violated this policy. A friend introduced me to a girl who was so pretty, I could never have forgotten meeting her. So when my friend asked, "Jacob, do you know Anita?" I stuck out my hand and said, with all the suave confidence I could muster, "No, I don't. It's a pleasure to meet you."

Anita stared at me in disbelief. "This is the third time we've met this month," she said.

Oops.

Now, maybe you're thinking, *That just proves Jacob and Anita weren't meant to be. If it was true love, he would have remembered meeting her.*

But the same thing happened to me with another girl, named Lauren. We met in college . . . or so I thought. She remembers meeting me several years earlier. Fortunately, she must not have been too bothered by my absentmindedness, because we ended up getting married.

Remembering people's names should be a simple matter of applying the techniques we've already learned.

Find a distinctive feature. Then chunk that feature together with a vivid image that suggests the name.

You could imagine a big rose growing out of this girl's hair.

LOCK
57

You could imagine this boy's ear running off his head to meet its all-time favorite author, Jacob Sager Weinstein.

In theory, using these techniques to memorize names isn't any harder than using them to memorize anything else. In practice, I find names to be my greatest challenge. Shopping lists don't mind if I stare at them for a few minutes while I move them into my memory palace. Phone numbers won't be hurt if I say the wrong thing. But people are complicated, fast-moving creatures, and amid the pressures of meeting them, their names have a tendency to vanish moments after I've shaken their hands.

Fortunately I've got a couple of bonus techniques I deploy to help me out:

- If I'm entering a place where I'm likely to meet new people, I take a moment to note what the room looks like. Then I can use it as a memory palace to store my mnemonic images for the day. The real-life association between the place and the people I meet there helps the images stick.

- If I have the chance before we start speaking, I ask myself some goofy questions about the person: If they're secretly a superhero, what is their power? If they're a famous person in disguise, who are they? If they're a were-creature, what animal do they turn into? It's a fun, low-pressure way to start noticing things about their faces. IMPORTANT: Answer these questions silently. Shouting "You're a were-parrot!" won't make the best first impression.

- I repeat names as early and as often as I can without seeming weird.

Mnemonics

Now YOU Try It!

Because there's so much else to think about when you're meeting somebody, it's a good idea to have as many mnemonics prepared in advance as you possibly can. Here are ten common names. Can you match them to the images I use?

Elizabeth	Jennifer	Sofia	Sarah	Michael
Ahmed	José	Robert	Mary	William

Of course, those might not be the best images for you—feel free to make up your own. And if you want to be even more prepared, appendix C has a list of a hundred common names. Can you come up with images for them?

ELBOW

Answer Key

MICHAEL
A mic in an L

AHMED
"Ah!" + med(icine)

JENNIFER
Chin of fur

ROBERT
A robber

MARY
Mary had a little lamb

JOSÉ
hose A

ELIZABETH
Queen Elizabeth II

SARAH
Say "Rah!"

SOFIA
sew + fee

WILLIAM
William Tell shooting an arrow
through an apple

What We Learned in CHAPTER 7

ANSWER KEY | FAKE ITEM: 2

Now YOU Try It!

Names and Faces

Learn the following people's names. Then turn the page and test yourself.

Peter

Ryan

Saul

Beth

Adam

Aisha

Felicity

Phillip

Anna

Santiago

Reza

Mei

Josephina

Caroline

Patty

Joseph

8
Bun, Shoe, Tree, Door: An Introduction to Remembering Numbers

We've seen it again and again: the more abstract something is, the harder it is to remember. And numbers are as abstract as you can get. Just try coming up with a vivid, multisensory image for 913,291,091,432. What does it sound like when 9 crashes into 13? How does 291 smell? What's funny or strange about 091,432?

Fortunately, there's a system for converting numbers into concrete, vivid images. In fact, there are a whole bunch of systems.

The easiest is to come up with a rhyme for each digit:

0: Nero

1: Bun

2: Shoe

3: Tree

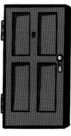

4: Door

5: Hive

6: Sticks

7: Heaven

8: Plate

9: Sign

You can use these images the way you'd use any others. You can store them in memory palaces. You can chunk them together with other images.

The Huang He, also called the Yellow River, is the sixth-longest river in the world.

If you need to remember a number above 10, you just chunk these images together. To remember **309**, you'd picture this:

If you don't need to remember more than three digits at a time, number rhymes will serve you just fine. But the longer the number, the more unwieldy this method gets. Your image for **4,262,694** is going to look like this:

JAIL

65

There's no reason you can't remember that, but there are two potential drawbacks. First, the repeated elements make you more likely to run into interference. Fortunately, if you carefully imagine that shoe interacting in a different way with each distinctive location, you can overcome that.

More challengingly, that memory walk is on the long side—you've burned seven locations to learn a single number. If you memorize a lot of long numbers, the rhyming system might grow unwieldy. In Part II of this book, we'll discuss an advanced way of learning long numbers—the same system world-class memory athletes use to memorize thousands of digits at a time. But if this chapter's rhyming system does the trick for you, there's no need to dive into deeper waters.

What We Learned in CHAPTER 8

1. Simple rhymes to replace digits with more concrete images
2. A short poem to remember those rhymes
3. Potential drawbacks of the rhyme system

ANSWER KEY | FAKE ITEM: 2

Now YOU Try It!

The Elements

Try using number rhymes to remember the number of each of these elements in the periodic table:

Hydrogen	•	1
Oxygen	•	8
Chlorine	•	17
Calcium	•	20

Iron	•	26
Silver	•	47
Gold	•	79
Einsteinium	•	99

JUG
66

Now YOU Try It!

What is the number of each of the following elements?

Silver
Gold
Calcium
Oxygen
Chlorine
Hydrogen
Iron
Einsteinium

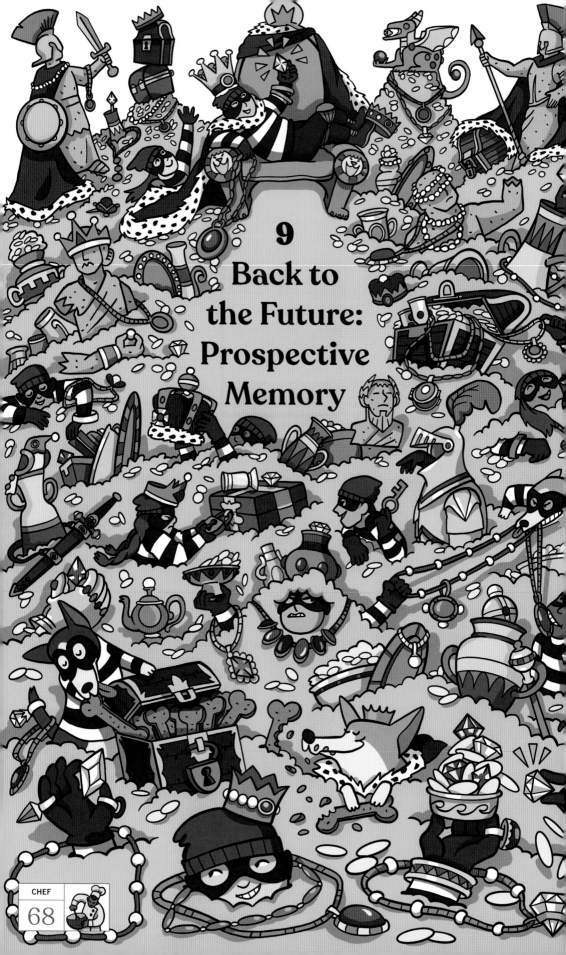

9
Back to the Future: Prospective Memory

So far, we've talked about remembering things that have already happened. Believe it or not, that's not the only kind of memory there is.

RETROSPECTIVE VS. PROSPECTIVE MEMORY

Retrospective memory is remembering stuff from the past. It's what most people think of as "memory."

Prospective memory is remembering to do stuff in the future.

Even if you've never heard of it until now, you've used prospective memory all your life. You use it every time you remember to put on your pants before leaving the house, or you remember to meet someone for dinner. And it's failed you every time you've forgotten to call your best friend on their birthday.

Imagine that you go into a party planning to use the Rose on Your Head technique to remember people's names. Half an hour later, though, you realize you didn't use it and you don't know who anybody is! It will feel like your **retrospective** memory has let you down, but the real culprit might be your **prospective** memory. Did you learn people's names and then forget them—or did you forget to learn them in the first place?

To help us improve our prospective memory, it's worth thinking about the times when it works well. How come you never forget to put on your clothes before going outside? Most people rely on two kinds of hints, or *cues*:

1. Natural cues (like being cold when you're naked)
2. Ritual cues (like always getting dressed when you get out of the shower)

GOOP

69

Cues are just another kind of chunking. With natural cues, the world does the chunking for you. Your stomach rumbles when you're hungry, whether you want it to or not!

And rituals are a way of gradually chunking things yourself, over time. You weren't born with an association between getting in a car and buckling your seat belt, but by now you've done both things so often that you can't imagine one without the other.[3]

If your prospective memory is letting you down, it's because there isn't a strong enough link between the thing you want to do and the time or place you want to do it. You just need to chunk those things together.

Suppose you're the queen of England. (Hey, I never know who's going to be reading my book!) Tomorrow is the annual opening of Parliament, and you must remember to put on your very best Crown Jewels before leaving the palace. Unfortunately, there are no natural cues for this—walking outside with your casual diamond tiara feels exactly the same as walking outside with your best-quality crown. And an annual opening doesn't happen often enough to establish a ritual cue.

Somehow, though, you must chunk "putting on the Crown Jewels" with "leaving the palace." There are four kinds of cues you might use:

1. **Linking Cue:** Every day before leaving the palace, you give each of your dogs a delicious Royal Doggie Biscuit. It's a habit as deeply ingrained as brushing your teeth. By leaving the Crown Jewels next to the antique crystal vase in which the RDBs are stored, you can link something you might not remember to something you definitely will.

3. Or so I hope! I can't afford to lose a reader.

2. **Abstract Cue:** As a loyal (and royal) fan of the *Wimpy Kid* books, you imitate your personal hero Greg Heffley by throwing a pillow against the door of your bedroom. In the morning, you'll notice the pillow is out of place, and that will trigger your memory.

3. **Intentional Cue:** You simply form a clear intention in your mind: "When we put on our coat tomorrow, we will also put on our best Crown Jewels." (The best part of being queen is that you get to use the royal *we*.)

4. **Enactment Cue:** Just to make sure the intention sticks, you physically act out the behavior you want to remember. You imagine it's the next morning, and you mime putting on your royal coat. You sit on the floor and mime putting on your royal shoes. Then you stand up and mime putting on the Crown Jewels, picturing them vividly in your mind as you do so.

Even if you're not the queen of England, you've probably used some of those cues (although you might not have known what to call them). You might have created a *linking cue* by putting a permission slip on top of a school backpack. You might have created an *abstract cue* by tying a string around your finger. You might have created an *intentional cue* by thinking, *When I get home, I'll throw my stinky socks in the laundry.*

COAT

All of those are helpful. Studies have shown that even the simple act of creating an intentional cue—of resolving to do action A when you do action B—can help you remember to do something.

But you probably haven't used an *enactment cue*, and that's a pity. As silly as it seems, miming the actions you want to remember has been scientifically shown to help you remember them.

The Science Behind the Technique

Neurons that fire together wire together. In other words, if you activate two parts of your brain at the same time, it creates a connection. The next time you fire up one of those parts, there's a good chance the other one will fire up as well.

When you imagine something vividly enough, you fire up some of the same neurons you would if you were actually doing it— especially if you act out the physical actions associated with it. When you mime opening your  front door and then hanging your keys on a hook before you lose them, you fire the door-opening neurons and the key-hanging neurons together. When you open your front door in reality, your key-hanging circuits are likely to fire up again.

If you've watched the Winter Olympics, you've seen the power of this technique. Before her run, a skier will often stand with her eyes closed, rocking back and forth as if she were already skiing. In a moment she's going to put her prospective memory to a grueling test: she's going to have to lean in precisely the right direction at precisely the right moment as she shoots through the snow. By miming her response to every curve of the course, she's giving herself a series of enactment cues. If they can stop her from plowing headfirst into a mogul at eighty miles an hour, they can definitely help you remember to hang up those keys.

1. The difference between prospective memory and retrospective memory (What is it?)

2. The difference between a natural cue and a ritual cue (What is it?)

3. Linking cues, abstract cues, intentional cues, and enactment cues: What are they and how are they used?

4. How chronological cues can interfere with geographical cues

5. How world-class athletes use enactment cues

ANSWER KEY | FAKE ITEM: 4

Now YOU Try It!

Tap Your Nose

The test for this chapter is a little different: when you get to the end of the next chapter, tap your nose three times.

COMB

10
The Fickle Hippo of Memory: Retaining Memories for the Long Term

I n the previous chapters, we've practiced all kinds of techniques for getting stuff into your memory. Now it's time for another challenge: keeping it there.

To put it more scientifically, we need to make sure that the things we've put in our short-term memory end up tucked safely away in our long-term memory.

SHORT-TERM AND LONG-TERM MEMORY

Short-term memory is where your brain stores the stuff it needs to know at this very moment, like "My hair is currently on fire."

Long-term memory is where your brain stores the stuff it expects to need in the future, like "Never make a dragon sneeze."

If you want to make sure you've learned something, one method would be to sit at your desk for an hour and reread it again and again. Among people who haven't studied the mnemonic arts, this is a popular option. If you repeat a phrase to yourself over and over, you are pretty much guaranteed to cram it into your memory.

The only problem is, you've crammed it into your *short-term* memory. Imagine this is your brain.

When you memorize something, it's like scribbling it on a note and putting it in the Mailbox of Short-Term Memory.

If you cram for an hour, you're taking that note out of the mailbox and putting it back, over and over again. By the end of that hour, you will have mastered the art of putting it there. You'll feel like you've got that material down cold.

But you don't. No matter how many times you put it into the short-term mailbox, it'll never be the same as putting it into the Big House of Long-Term Memory.

So how *does* that note get into your long-term memory? Every once in a while, a part of your brain called the *hippocampus* toddles over, looks at everything in the mailbox, and grabs the notes it thinks are important. It brings those back to the house. And everything else?

Gone forever.

Fortunately, there are certain things your hippocampus is more likely to take into the Big House of Long-Term Memory: things that are strange or shocking or funny, striking images, stories, and the details of places you've visited. It's no coincidence that these are exactly the things mnemonic techniques tend to rely on.

So if you use these techniques, are you guaranteed to remember everything forever?

Alas, no. Your hippocampus tucks those memory notes in a million different places. Sometimes when you forget something, the note is still there, but your hippocampus doesn't know where to find it.

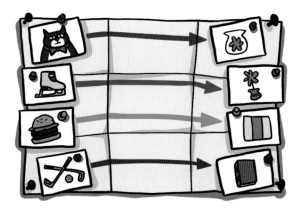

The good news is, linking memories to vivid images makes them much easier to find.

A completely scientific depiction of your hippocampus at work.

CAKE
77

The bad news is, even the most vivid mental map is going to fade over time. And when it does, your hippocampus can't retrieve the memories.

The good news is, every time you force your brain to go into its stacks and pull out a memory, it adds another layer of ink to that map, so it will fade more slowly.

IMPORTANT: For this to work, you have to force your brain to pull the fact out. You can't just reread the sentence "There are 206 bones in the human body." You have to ask yourself, "How many bones are there in the human body?" and then remember "206."

Or, to put it another way: you can't just *reread*. You have to *retest*. That's what makes your hippocampus do the hard work of redrawing the map.

MASSED REPETITION & SPACED REPETITION

When you put something into your short-term memory over and over again without a break, it's called **massed repetition**. (At least, that's what scientists call it. Most people call it "cramming.")

When you give your brain some time to transfer things to your long-term memory before pulling them out again, it's called **spaced repetition**. It feels harder, because you're constantly dancing on the edge of forgetting. But it's much more effective at sealing things into your brain.

You could capitalize on this by quizzing yourself on everything every day for the rest of your life. You'd never forget anything. You'd also never have any free time.

Imagine, though, that you could retest a memory precisely one second before the map to it fades. You'd never forget anything—and you'd never waste a moment retesting something you didn't need to. Plus, the very fact that the memory was nearly lost would make your hippocampus engrave it just a little more carefully.

Unless you're reading this book in the year 2072, when it probably comes with brain-scanning technology, I can't tell you how to time things quite that precisely. The strength of the map depends on your particular brain and how strong an impression the memory made in the first place. But as a starting schedule, retest yourself on most things after:

Ten minutes One day Four days One week One month Three months Six months Nine months One year

Retesting yourself at these intervals is easier said than done. On top of remembering whatever it is you're remembering, you have to remember when you last retested it, and how many times you retested it before that, and when you're supposed to retest it next. And you've got to do all that on a schedule specifically designed to take you right up to the edge of forgetting.

So let's make things a little easier. You'll still remember the thing you're memorizing, whether it's French vocabulary or the birthdays of everybody in your class—but you're going to let a bunch of index cards remember the schedule you're learning it on.

You could use actual, real-life paper index cards. Practitioners of spaced repetition have used them for more than a century. In appendix A, I'll tell you how to make a box that keeps track of when you're supposed to retest each card. If you don't have access to a computer or smartphone, it's a great method—and well worth the effort of setting it up.

But if you can use an index card app, you will save yourself some trouble. Plus, as a bonus, a good app will tweak the timing of each card depending on how often you get it wrong. You'll see the hard cards more often than the easy ones.

Which app you use depends on your computer hardware (not to mention your mental hardware!). Everybody's brain is different—and everybody's phone/computer/tablet is, too. Just search your app store for "flash cards" or "spaced repetition" and play around with the options until you find one you like.

Whatever flash card system you use—virtual or real-world—they all work more or less the same way: You look at one side of a card. You guess the answer, and then you turn over the card. You tell the system whether you got it right or wrong. (Some systems have more options, like "I got it right, but it was really hard," or "DUH! Obviously I know this.") If you got it right, great! The system waits longer to show it to you next time. And if you got it wrong, no worries! The system puts it back in the pile of stuff you need to review. Either way, you've fixed it a little more firmly in your memory. Then you go on to the next card.

What flag is this?

And that's it. This book is full of ingenious and increasingly complicated ways to remember stuff, and "Put it on index cards" is a lot less glamorous than "Imagine George Washington arm-wrestling a gibbon." But *retesting beats rereading* and *spaced repetition beats massed repetition* are two of the most important concepts I can teach you. Tons of scientific research has shown that spaced repetition is the best way to keep things in your brain, yet most of humanity carries on cramming and forgetting.

This simple concept is so important, I'm going to make it the Third Rule of Memory: **The best way to keep stuff in your brain is to test yourself on it with spaced repetition.**

Even better, let's make the Third Rule follow its own guidelines:

The best way to keep stuff in your brain is to ___ yourself on it with ___.

And now you know why I've put lots of questions (and one fake fact!) into the review section of every chapter. If you've been playing along, you've been regularly reaching into your brain, pulling stuff out, and comparing it to the things I claimed we discussed.

VASE

80

1. Why retesting is better than rereading (Why is it?)

2. Why it's helpful to retest yourself at steadily increasing intervals (Why is it?)

3. Why retesting is better than rereading (Why is it?)

4. The difference between spaced repetition and massed repetition (What is it?)

5. Why retesting is better than rereading (Why is it?)

6. The Third Rule of Memory (What is it?)

7. The difference between short-term memory and long-term memory (What is it?)

8. A rough schedule for spaced repetition

9. The role your hippocampus plays in storing and retrieving memories

10. Why retesting is better than getting punched in the nose

ANSWER KEY | FAKE ITEM:10

Now YOU Try It!

Prospective Memory

Since this chapter is about long-term memory, I'm not going to test the skills you just learned.

But I *did* just test your prospective memory. If you tapped your nose three times, you passed.

FOOT

11
Speaking of Retesting: What Were We Saying About Retesting?

You've now learned the basics of every memory technique I know. The rest of the book will teach you how to use those techniques for all kinds of cool stuff. First, though, we're going to review those basics.

If you've been paying attention, I think you'll know the answer to most of these questions. But if not, don't worry! I've included the page number for every answer. Either way, by telling your hippocampus to go root around in your brain for this information, you're fixing it more firmly in your memory.

What is the First Rule of Memory? (page 9)

What is chunking? (page 6)

What is the Second Rule of Memory? (page 12)

What makes an image memorable? (pages 10–12)

What is the memory palace method? (page 29–31)

What kinds of places can you use as memory palaces? (page 37)

How many kinds of verbal mnemonics can you list? (page 43–48)

What is the difference between *prospective memory* and *retrospective memory*? (page 69)

What is the difference between *spaced repetition* and *massed repetition*, and which is better? (page 78)

What technique did we learn for memorizing numbers? What are the strengths and weaknesses of that technique? (pages 64–66)

What is the Third Rule of Memory? (page 80)

Give one example of something you might memorize with each of the following techniques: chunking, a memory palace, a verbal mnemonic, and the story method.

FOAM

83

12
The International Number Mafia: Remembering Longer Numbers

If you just have to remember a few digits at a time, the rhyme method from chapter 8 will do the trick. But if you want to memorize longer numbers, it's worth taking the time to memorize something called the Major System. The Major System is going to take more work to learn than any of the techniques we've discussed so far—but if you put in the time and effort, you can accomplish amazing things.

Amnazing Mnemonic Mnasters

In March 2015, Rajveer Meena set a world record by reciting 70,000 digits of pi from memory. It took him almost ten hours to recite them all.

As we discussed in the very first chapter, words are easier to remember than letters—"chocolate" is easier to remember than *a, e, c, h, o, o, c, l, t*. And numbers are just another kind of letter. If only they made sounds, you could make them into words, too.

Well, the International Number Mafia doesn't want me to tell you this, but every number *does* have a sound. Some of them even have two! So all you need to do is—LOOK OUT! It's the number 38, wielding a rotten tomato! The International Number Mafia is onto us! DUCK!!

VIAL
85

Okay, I confess. There's no such thing as the International Number Mafia. But there *are* secret sounds for each letter. Here they are, along with tips for remembering them:

0	Z or S	"Zero" starts with *Z*. But *Z* is a pretty rare letter, so we'll throw in the similar-sounding *S*.
1	T or D	1 looks kind of like a *T*. *T* and *D* sound very similar.
2	N	A 2 on its side looks like an *N*.
3	M	A 3 on its side looks like an *M*.
4	R	"Four" ends with *r*.
5	L	*L* is the Roman numeral for 50.
6	G or SH or CH or J	A 6 looks like a *G*. Depending on the word, *G* can sound like *SH* or *CH* or *J*.
7	K	A *K* looks like two 7s stacked on top of each other.
8	F or V	If you join up the ends of a lowercase *f*, you get an 8. *V* sounds almost like *F*.
9	P or B	Turn 9 backward and it becomes a *P*. Rotate it, and it becomes a *b*.

Admittedly, those sounds are all pretty arbitrary. But they're a major help if you want to remember numbers. That's why mnemonists call it "the Major System"!

Suppose you need to remember 92. 9 is P and 2 is N, so 92 is "PN."

That's still not very easy to remember. But here's something cool about the Major System: no digit gets turned into a vowel—not even a *Y*. That means you won't change the number if you add as many vowels as you need to make a sensible word. So 92 could be "pin," "pan," "open," or even "piano." And if your best friend's name is Aeeeaiupoøéinia, that would be 92 also. For that matter, no digit gets turned into *W* or *H*, so Aeeeaiupoøéinia's brother Aaahyaaaaaawpno is still 92.

Let's try some other numbers.

10 = TS. Add a few vowels and we've got "tease" or "oats."

43 = RM. That could be "room," "Romeo," or "ram."

38 = MF. That could be "mafia"—WATCH OUT!

The Major System is based on sound, not spelling. So "no" and "knee" both equal the number 2. "Knee" has an extra *K*, but it's a silent letter. If you don't pronounce it, you don't translate it into digits. And "Otto" has two *T*s, but only one *T sound*, so "Otto" equals 1. And "Mac" is 37 (because the *c* is pronounced like *k*) but "mice" is 30 (because the *c* is pronounced like *s*).

That might seem confusing at first, but it means you don't have to worry about spelling a word correctly. For most people, the tradeoff is worth it. But if you want to think about spelling instead of sound—if you want to treat "knee" as 72 and "Otto" as 11—you can! Remember the Second Law of Memory: *Everybody's brain is different.* The Major System has been tweaked in various ways since it was invented, and there's no reason you can't tweak it to suit yourself.

Just make sure you're consistent. Always use the sound, or always use the spelling, but don't switch back and forth or you'll only confuse yourself.

If you're a highly verbal person, you can convert numbers to words whenever you see them. But if that's too hard—or if you just want to save yourself time down the road—you can memorize a word for each number from 0 to 99 and have them ready to go.

FAKE
87

In fact, take a look at the bottom of this very page. You'll see the page number and, right next to it, a little picture of a "fife." Fife is 88 in the Major System. This is page 88. Every page in this book has an appropriate illustration next to the page number. You could chunk that image to the contents of the page and *memorize the entire book*. Who needs an index? I'll just glue *you* to the binding, and you can tell people where to find things!

If you don't want to have to flip through every page in the book to look up Major System words, just to turn to appendix B for a whole list of them in one place.

Whether you memorize your Major System words in advance or just memorize the number sounds and make up the words on the spot, you can assign a vivid, easily imaginable word to every number between 1 and 100. Then you can link those words to . . . well, anything you want to know a number for. Want to remember the uniform numbers of your favorite basketball players? Just picture #23 Michael Jordan watching anime. And next to him, #30 Steph Curry dunks on a mouse.

Or perhaps you'd rather remember the presidents. Just picture Abraham Lincoln, the 16th president, playing tag, while #35 John F. Kennedy delivers the mail.

Of course, you can use the Major System to remember numbers with more than two digits. We'll talk about how to do that in the next chapter.

Now YOU Try It!

Numbers

But first, let's practice. Can you identify the following numbers? You can check your answers by turning to the page with that number and seeing if the image is there.

1. Using the Major System to assign a sound to the numbers 0–9

2. Adding vowels to make any number into a word

3. The number that represents the International Number Mafia (What is it?)

4. What the little pictures next to the page numbers in this book mean

5. How Gregor von Feinaigle used this system to memorize 10,000 digits of pi

6. How long it takes to recite 70,000 digits of pi

ANSWER KEY | FAKE ITEM: 5

Now YOU Try It!

Dates and Events

Use the Major System to remember the years these events happened:

Event	Year
First phase of the construction of Stonehenge	3000 BC
Building begins on the Pyramid of Djoser, perhaps the oldest pyramid in Egypt	2667 BC
Rome founded, according to legend	753 BC
Magna Carta signed	AD 1215
French Revolution begins	1789
Einstein's Theory of General Relativity published	1915
Humans first walk on the Moon	1969

What years did the following events occur?

First phase of the construction of Stonehenge
Building begins on the Pyramid of Djoser, perhaps the oldest pyramid in Egypt
Rome founded, according to legend
Magna Carta signed
French Revolution begins
Einstein's Theory of General Relativity published
Humans first walk on the Moon

13
Ice Cream and Hot Fudge: Combining Techniques

I know what you're saying: "I can already memorize the presidents in order using a memory palace. Why do I need to learn a whole new system?"[4]

First, the Major System is *random access*, which means you can easily jump to any entry. If you want to know who the 32nd president is, you don't have to start at George Washington and walk through your palace counting presidents. You can immediately jump to FDR, wearing a lion's mane.

Second, the Major System and the memory palace are like peanut butter and jelly, or ice cream and hot fudge: they're good individually, but when you combine them, you get something even better. Now that you don't have to store the presidents inside your memory palace in the order they served, you can organize them any way you want. You could put all the one-termers on the first floor, and all the two-termers on the second, and put FDR triumphantly on the roof.

If you want to get really fancy, you can combine the Major System and a memory palace *and* standard modifications. Use the Major System to remember the order of the presidents. As a standard modification, put a dunce cap on all the presidents who lost reelection, and a gold medal on all the ones who served a second term. Put the Democrats on the first floor, the Republicans on the second, and the Democratic-Republicans on the staircase between floors. You've now tripled the information you've stored in a single mind palace.

For that matter, you can combine the Major System with *any* technique in this book. Once you've converted numbers into words, you can remember those words with a verbal mnemonic or a story just as well as with a picture.

This is especially useful when you're dealing with long numbers. If you wanted to remember 913,291,091,432, you could just transform the whole thing into one phrase. Let's see . . . if we swap in each digit for a letter, we get BTMNBTSPDRMN. Add a couple of A's, an occasional O or U, an E, and we've got . . .

BaTMaN BeaT SPiDeR-MaN.

Woo-hoo! We already memorized that back in chapter 1! What an incredible coincidence!

---

4. Unless you're saying, "Help! I'm being eaten by a bear!" If so, try to wedge his jaws open long enough to read my next book, How to Avoid Getting Eaten by Anything.

Unfortunately, most numbers won't just happen to spell a convenient phrase. Fortunately, any number, no matter how long, can be broken down into a bunch of two-digit pairs (possibly with one extra digit at the beginning or end). As you break it down into those pairs, you just take a word associated with each pair and store it in your memory palace.

Suppose your Social Security number is **982-47-6825**. Here's how that might look inside your brain:

The bad news is that long numbers can rapidly use up locations in your memory palace. The good news is that you can squeeze multiple numbers into a single location:

Not only does this save space in your palace, but you might find it's faster, too. You wouldn't think walking from one location in your palace to the next would take time, but many mnemonists find it does.

For that reason, master mnemonists don't just learn one word for each number. They learn *three*: **a person**, **an action**, **and an object**. Whenever they picture a sequence of numbers, they picture the person[5] for the first number, the action for the second, and the object for the third.

165,711:
DJ = 16
LicK = 57
TaTtoo = 11

111,657:
DiG = 16
TeDdy = 11
LocK = 57

571,116:
LuKe = 57
ToTe = 11
TaG = 16

5. As you can see, my definition of "people" includes teddy bears.

If you have a **p**erson, an **a**ction, and an **o**bject, that's called a PAO system.

If you have a person, an action, and an object for every number from 0 to 99, that's called a *century* PAO system.

Some memory masters have a *millennium* PAO— they've learned a person, an action, and an object for every number from 0 to 999! If you want to set a world record for memorizing pi, you'll probably need a millennium PAO. But for most ordinary uses, a century PAO is plenty powerful.

1. How to combine the Major System with other memory techniques

2. What PAO stands for (What does it stand for?)

3. Why a PAO system can be faster

4. The difference between a century PAO and an eon PAO

ANSWER KEY | FAKE ITEM: 4

Now YOU Try It!

British Monarchs

Here are eight British monarchs. Remember the house of each one by using a standard modification, or by putting the Tudors, Yorks, and Stuarts in separate rooms of a memory palace.

Use the Major System to remember the year they took the throne.

HOUSE OF YORK	HOUSE OF TUDOR	HOUSE OF STUART
Edward IV (1461)	Henry VIII (1509)	James I (1603)
Richard III (1483)	Mary I (1553)	Charles I (1625)
	Elizabeth I (1558)	Anne (1702)

What year did each of the following monarchs
take the throne, and what house were they of?

Edward IV
Richard III
Henry VIII
Mary I
Elizabeth I
James I
Charles I
Anne

14
Mr. Rogers Gift-Wrapping a Dog:
Remembering Your Entire Life

Dates are just numbers, and if you only need to remember them occasionally, you can use any of the methods we've already discussed.

Remembering 9/3/94

The Number Rhyme System

sign = 9   knee = 3   sign = 9   door = 4

The Major System

ape = 9   mow = 3   brow = 94

The Numbers-Wearing-Funny-Hats System[6]

But if you're willing to learn a special system for dates, you can do something *amazing*. You can pull off the greatest memory trick in the world: You can remember your own life.

Of all the frustrations that come with my monkeybrain, the greatest has

6. Not an actual system. I'm just seeing if you're paying attention.

been feeling that my past has slipped away from me. I'm annoyed that I can't remember all those facts I crammed into my head in grade school. But I'm *mournful* that I've forgotten so much of what I felt and did in the hours I wasn't cramming.

After forty-six years of forgetting, I decided to do something about it by choosing one moment from each day to remember forever. Maybe it's something low-key, like playing a board game with my kids. Maybe it's something big, like my cousin's wedding. Whatever it is, I consciously store it away. It takes a moment— but it lasts a lifetime.

To do so, I use a special PAO (Person Action Object) system.

A PAO system has two advantages. First, it lets us compress more information into a single image. And second, it makes us less

PAO

If you've read chapter 13, you already know all about PAO, but as a quick refresher:

In a Person Action Object system, each image has three parts. You'll *never* guess what they are!

Wait, did you guess "Person, action, and object"? Huh. You're right.

likely to mix up what the images represent. For example, in a PAO for numbers, we always know that the person will represent the first digit, the action will be the second digit, and the object will be the third.

By contrast, in our PAO for dates, the person always represents the year; the action always represents the month; and the object always represents the day.

If you've already memorized a century PAO—that is, the people, actions, and objects for the numbers 0 to 99—you could simply use that. But when I'm storing the days of my life in a treasure house, I want to be extra careful not to lose them, and that means minimizing interference. So I've got a series of images I use only for my personal memories.

For dates, I've selected thirty-one objects based on the Major System—a different set of Major System objects from the ones I usually use. I won't list them here; if you want suggestions, take a look at the Major System chart in appendix B.

For each month, I've chosen an action that's easy to picture and (at least for me) associated with that month:

JANUARY
popping a champagne cork at

FEBRUARY
kissing

MARCH
marching on

APRIL
putting a whoopee cushion under

MAY
plucking a flower

JUNE
riding a roller coaster with

JULY
shooting fireworks at

AUGUST
applying sunscreen

SEPTEMBER
putting into a school backpack

OCTOBER
trick-or-treating with

NOVEMBER
stuffing into a turkey

DECEMBER
wrapping in gift paper

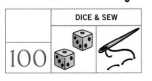

DICE & SEW

100

And as for the year . . . Well, here's where I get a bit creative.

If I was just memorizing regular dates, I might use whatever person the Major System assigned. For 2021, I just need to remember 21.[7] I could use my friend Nat.

But that means Nat will make a guest appearance in every memory I create for the year. On New Year's Day 2022, if Nat gets arrested for robbing a bank, my entire 2021 will be retroactively tainted by his villainy. That *probably* won't happen. Nat certainly *seems* nice. But am I willing to bet my whole year on it?

Let me take a step back. Why did I even need to use the Major System in choosing the avatar of 2021? The advantage of the Major System is that it helps you remember which number is associated with which image—but whoever I choose for 2021, I'm going to picture that person every day for the entire year. Even for a monkeybrain like me, that's enough time to make the connection stick.

Therefore, I can safely ignore the Major System and just choose anybody I like as my Person of the Year. To make sure they stay out of trouble, I choose people who are fictional or deceased. One year, it might be Leonardo da Vinci. The next, it might be Mary Poppins. Neither of them is ever going to get caught dynamiting their way into a high-security vault!

But everybody's brain is different. Maybe for you, the risk of forgetting who your Person of the Year is outweighs the risk of discovering they're a bank robber. If so, feel free to use the Major System (or any other system) to choose your Person of the Year.

Now that I've chosen my images, using them might go something like this. It's **December 16, 2018**. I look back on my day and decide to remember my wife's choir concert.

7. It's not like I'm going to think one of my personal memories took place in 1921. I'm not that old!

DICE & TEA

101

The year 2018 was "Mr. Rogers." December is "wrapping in gift paper." And 16 is "dog." So I imagine the scene this way:

Right now, you're probably saying, "But isn't the whole point to remember your actual life? You're deliberately changing your own memories!"

It turns out that, absentminded though I am, I'm able to tell the difference between real memories and mnemonic devices. When I ask myself what I was doing on December 16, 2018, I think of Mr. Rogers and his gift-wrapped dog, and I see that goofy image—and then I can immediately shift to all the real images from that night.

It's as though my hippocampus keeps the original memory and simply uses the crazy image I've concocted as a map to find it.

What We
Learned in
CHAPTER
14

1. A PAO system for dates

2. The date George Washington crossed the Delaware (When was it?)

3. What kind of people I insert into my memories

Now YOU Try It!

Dates and Events

Remember the dates of the following events.

Julius Caesar assassinated	March 15, 44 BC
The Battle of Hastings	October 14, AD 1066
William Shakespeare born	April 23, 1564
Darwin publishes *On the Origin of Species*	November 24, 1859
World War I begins	July 28, 1914
India gains independence	August 15, 1947
First *Harry Potter* book published	June 26, 1997

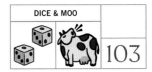

DICE & MOO

What are the dates of these events?

| Julius Caesar assassinated |
| The Battle of Hastings |
| William Shakespeare born |
| Darwin publishes *On the Origin of Species* |
| World War I begins |
| India gains independence |
| First *Harry Potter* book published |

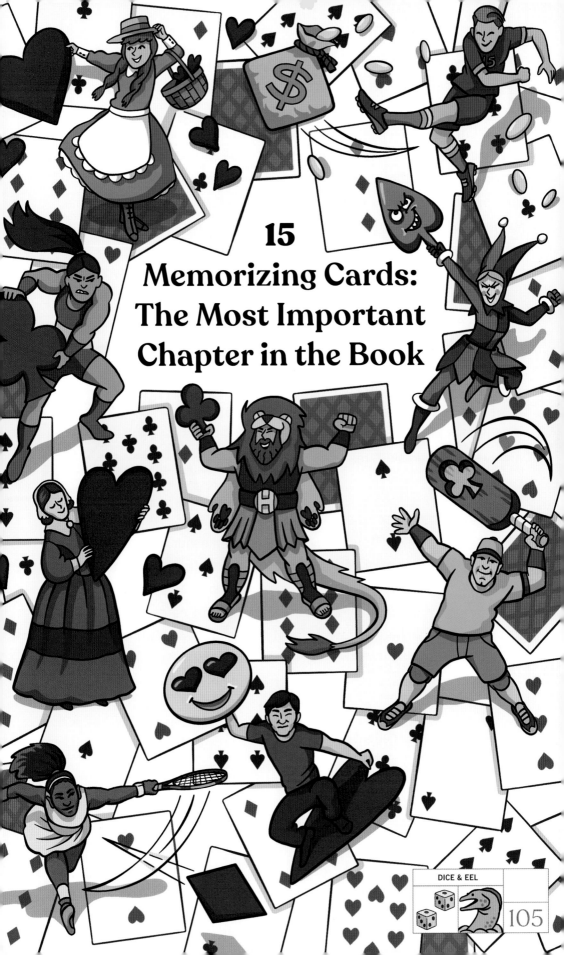

15
Memorizing Cards:
The Most Important
Chapter in the Book

I know what you're saying: "This isn't the most important chapter! Remembering to put your pants on before you leave the house is much more useful than memorizing a deck of cards."[8]

But I'm the youngest child of three. There are lots of advantages to being the youngest. (Trust me: you get away with MUCH more.) Unfortunately, you lose a lot of games—no matter how good you get, your big siblings always have a couple years' more practice. Being able to memorize cards wouldn't have helped me win Monopoly or Life, but it would have given me a major leg up in Go Fish or Gin.

Nowadays, my game-winning needs aren't quite so urgent. My wife and I are evenly matched, and I don't mind being beaten by my kids. But I still take a completely irrational pride in my ability to memorize a whole deck of cards. It's a way of proving to myself how far my mnemonic studies have taken me.

If you don't have card games to win or a point to prove, you're welcome to skip this chapter. But if you'd like to join me on the journey to this highly specialized skill, read on.

Amnazing Mnemonic Mnasters

In 2017, eighteen-year-old Munkhshur Narmandakh of Mongolia beat out competitors of all ages from twenty different countries to become World Memory Champion. She also set a world record for most cards memorized in an hour: 37 decks, or 1,924 cards. Meanwhile, her twin sister, Enkshur, set a new record for most binary digits memorized—5,445 zeros and ones, all in the correct order!

Still with me? Excellent!

DICE & SHOE

106

8. Unless you're saying, "Help! Wolves have stolen my passport!" Make sure you read my next book, <u>How to Stop Wolves from Stealing Everything</u>.

By now, you're very familiar with the First Rule of Memory: *The easiest way to remember something is to remember something easy.* As you'll see, memorizing cards is a lot like memorizing numbers. We'll start off with an abstract, hard-to-remember thing. We'll apply a clever system to convert it into a concrete, easy-to-visualize image. And then we'll store that image in a memory palace.

To start, we're going to assign each card a distinctive person. The nine of hearts and the nine of diamonds blur together in my mind—but I'm never going to confuse Abraham Lincoln with Henry Ford.

You could just look at each card, give it whatever identity seems appropriate, and drill yourself until you've memorized all fifty-two identities. Your sister wants to be a famous jewelry designer, so she becomes the queen of diamonds. Your dog has three little black patches that look like clubs, so he becomes the three of clubs. That's the method used by master mnemonist Dominic O'Brien.

The Dominic System (as it's called) clearly works for Dominic—he won the World Memory Championship eight times! But as the Second Rule of Memory tells us: *Everybody's brain is different.* Personally, I found it too hard to come up with an individual association for each card just by looking at it. So I turned to a system by a different master mnemonist: Ed Cooke. Ed has never placed first in the World Memory Championship, but he's one of 154 people in the world awarded the title of Grand Master of Memory by the World Memory Sports Council, so I think he has *some* idea of what he's talking about.

Ed's system also involves making each card into a person. But he starts with a series of rules that help you pinpoint what each card will be.

DICE & KEY

107

First are the rules for each of the four suits:

 A heart represents love. So the *hearts* will be people who are particularly kind or beloved (by you or by the world at large).

 A diamond represents wealth. So the *diamonds* will be rich people.

 A club is a big, heavy weapon. So the *clubs* will be strong or violent people.

 A spade is . . . well, frankly, it's just a weird shape. So the *spades* will be funny or weird people.

Then Ed moves on to the numbers. Odd-numbered cards are men; even-numbered cards are women. (You can remember this as "The boys were odd, but the girls got even.") That means that the three of diamonds will be a wealthy man, and the six of clubs will be a strong woman.

If that's enough to help you assign and remember identities for all fifty-two cards, you can go ahead and do so! But if you need a little more help, we can break the cards down into even more specific pairs:

Ace/Two:
Athletes or game show contestants.
(Because competitors are always trying to come in first.)

Three/Four:
Actors.
(Because some of the most famous movies end up being trilogies, sometimes with an extra movie afterward.)

Five/Six:
Comic book or cartoon characters.
 (Because a 5 looks a little bit like a cape, and a 6 looks a little bit like a superhero's muscular arm.)

Seven/Eight:
Characters from literature.

(Because a 7 looks like an open book, and an 8
looks like a scroll.)

Nine/Ten:
Historical figures.

(Because 9 and 10 are the highest digits cards can have, and historical
figures lived longer ago than anybody else.)

Jack:
A famous person named Jack.

Queen/King:
**A male/female team who worked together to become king and queen
of their field. They could be from any of the categories above (comic
characters, historical figures, etc.) or from an entirely different one.**

Those aren't exactly the same categories that Ed Cooke uses—I've
heeded the Second Rule of Memory and chosen categories that work for
me. They might not all work for you. Maybe you know more about cooking
than sports, and you want aces and twos to be famous chefs. Maybe you
don't have a vivid mental image of anybody named Jack, and you want to
imagine the Jacks as famous musicians instead. It's up to you! Take some
time to figure out categories you know well, and write them down in your
memory notebook.

Once you've got all your categories, you can combine them to choose a
person for each card. In my system, for example, hearts are kind people,
and threes are male actors. For the three of hearts, I'll use the famously
nice Tom Hanks. Eight of clubs is a violent or strong female literary
character. In my mind, that's the Wicked Witch of the West.

The following is a chart for my version of Ed Cooke's system. Of course,
Ed's chart would be different, and I'm sure yours will be different still.

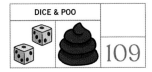

	Kind or beloved ♥
ACE (male competitor)	Jackie Robinson
TWO (female competitor)	Simone Biles
THREE (male actor)	Tom Hanks
FOUR (female actor)	Sandra Bullock
FIVE (male comic or cartoon character)	Captain America
SIX (female comic or cartoon character)	Wonder Woman
SEVEN (male literary character)	Dumbledore
EIGHT (female literary character)	Anne of Green Gables
NINE (male historical character)	Abraham Lincoln
TEN (female historical character)	Florence Nightingale
JACK	Jackie Chan
QUEEN	Ginger Rogers
KING	Fred Astaire

Wealthy ♦	Strong or violent ♣	Funny ♠
David Beckham	John Cena	Terry Crews
Serena Williams	Ronda Rousey	Megan Rapinoe
George Clooney	Arnold Schwarzenegger	Ken Jeong
Sofia Vergara	Michelle Rodriguez	Melissa McCarthy
Batman	The Hulk	Deadpool
Catwoman	She-Hulk	Harley Quinn
King Midas	Hercules	Willy Wonka
Cruella De Vil	Wicked Witch of the West	Alice in Wonderland
Henry Ford	Billy the Kid	Oscar Wilde
Cleopatra	Boudica	Jane Austen
Jack (of Jack and the Beanstalk)	Jack the Ripper	Captain Jack Sparrow
Beyoncé	Bonnie (of Bonnie & Clyde)	Lucille Ball
Jay-Z	Clyde	Desi Arnaz

TOTE & TEA

111

As you can see, Ed Cooke's system takes more work up front. You have to memorize the nature of the four suites and then the thirteen card values before you start picturing individual cards. I found that framework helpful, but the Second Rule of Memory tells me *you* might prefer the more freeform Dominic System.

However you choose the people for your cards, it's now time to memorize them. Eventually, you'll want to enter all those names into the flash cards (real or virtual) that you used for spaced repetition. But to start, I recommend you find an old, worn-out deck of cards (or splurge on a new one) and write the name of each person on the back of the appropriate card. Use that to quiz yourself until you're reasonably confident—having actual cards in your hand will give you a little bit of additional sensory detail.

Once you can look at the queen of diamonds and immediately think of Beyoncé, you're ready to start memorizing decks. All you need is a memory walk with at least fifty-two locations.

At first, this will be a slow process, but with practice, you'll improve.

Amnazing Mnemonic Mnasters

Shijir-Erdene Bat-Enkh of Mongolia can memorize cards faster than anybody else in the world—an entire deck in 12.74 seconds!

If you're just acquiring this skill to remember which cards are in the discard pile in Gin, you don't need to be especially fast. It takes me about ten minutes to memorize an entire deck, which works out to 11.5 seconds per card. That's good enough for most card games.

If you have dreams of competing in memory sports yourself, you're likely to need one more technique to get yourself up to speed. If you've read the chapters on dates and long numbers, you've already encountered it: it's the PAO system, or Person, Action, Object.

Review

In a PAO system, each image has three parts: a person, an action, and an object.

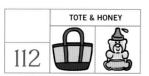

TOTE & HONEY

You've already worked out people for all fifty-two cards. Now you just need to come up with an action and an object associated with each person. Some of mine:

Card	Person	Action	Object
8♠	Alice in Wonderland	drinking	a bottle that says "Drink me"
5♣	The Hulk	smashing	torn cut-off jeans
Q♦	Beyoncé	doing the "Single Ladies" dance	a big diamond ring

If the first three cards in a deck were 8♠, 5♣, and the Q♦, I'd picture Alice smashing a diamond ring. If it was Q♦, 8♠, and 5♣, I'd picture Beyoncé drinking from a pair of torn jeans. (In case you're wondering how she does it: she dips the jeans in water, then squeezes them out.)

At first, you'll probably find it slower to generate these images than to just picture a sequence of people. But once you've got the images down cold—once you can look at the Q♦ and immediately see Beyoncé dancing with her ring finger up—you'll be amazed at how fast you can go.

Some people find it helpful to practice with a metronome. Start with a verrrrrrry slow rhythm, and try to memorize one card for each *tick*. Once you've mastered that, speed up the metronome and force yourself to go a little faster. If you get up to 245 beats per minute, congratulations—you just set a world record! Be sure to thank me in your teary acceptance speech at the World Memory Championships.

At the slower pace of twenty-six beats per minute, you can still learn an entire deck in two minutes. That's one of three qualifications to become an official International Master of Memory. Now you just need to memorize ten decks in an hour (a mere nine beats per minute) and one thousand random digits in an hour (seventeen digits per minute). International mastery, here you come!

TOTE & MOO

113

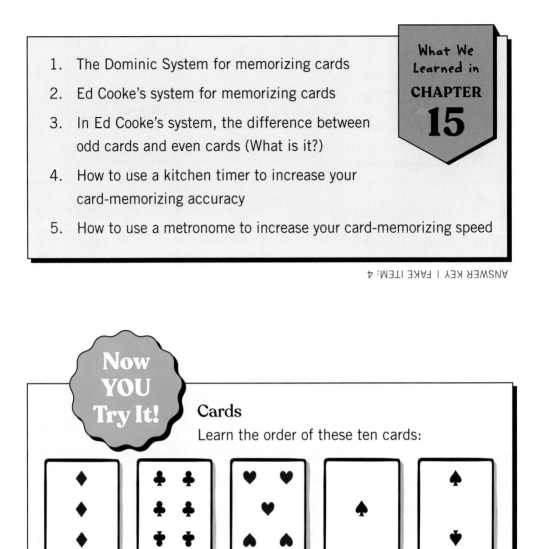

1. The Dominic System for memorizing cards

2. Ed Cooke's system for memorizing cards

3. In Ed Cooke's system, the difference between odd cards and even cards (What is it?)

4. How to use a kitchen timer to increase your card-memorizing accuracy

5. How to use a metronome to increase your card-memorizing speed

What We Learned in
CHAPTER
15

ANSWER KEY | FAKE ITEM: 4

Now YOU Try It!

Cards

Learn the order of these ten cards:

Cover up the ten cards you just memorized, and recite them.

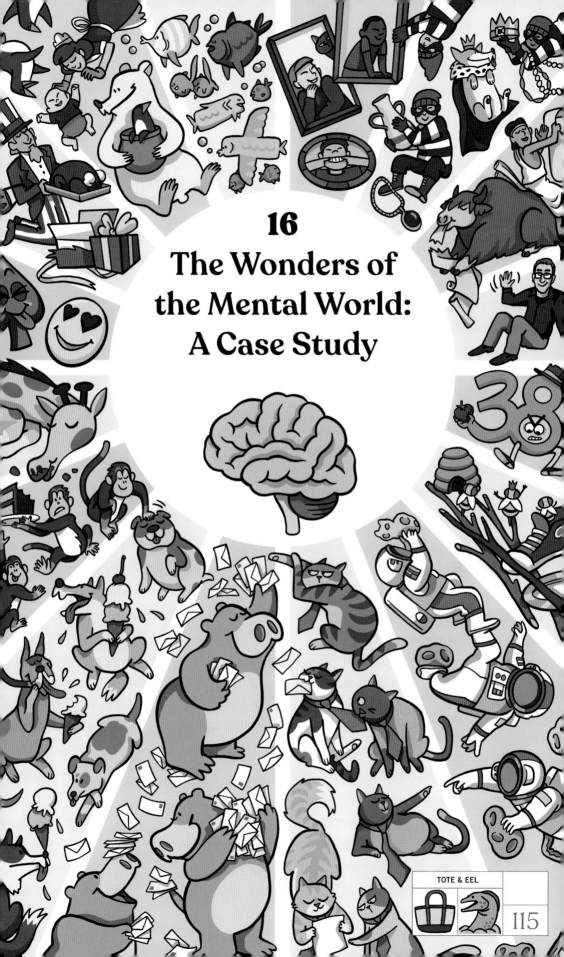

16
The Wonders of the Mental World:
A Case Study

O ver the past fifteen chapters, you've learned the secrets of ancient Roman orators and modern mental champions. You've taught yourself to build palaces in your mind and to preserve a lifetime's worth of memories.

It was, in short, an epic journey through the power of the human mind. Our final review ought to be equally epic. And so, to sum up many of the techniques we've studied, we're going to memorize the Seven Wonders of the Ancient World, in order of construction.

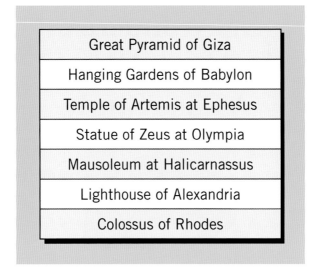

Great Pyramid of Giza
Hanging Gardens of Babylon
Temple of Artemis at Ephesus
Statue of Zeus at Olympia
Mausoleum at Halicarnassus
Lighthouse of Alexandria
Colossus of Rhodes

Seven items aren't too many, so I could construct a story mnemonic.[9]

One day, a mummy from a **great pyramid** was **hanging around the garden temple**. He saw his buddy **Zeus**, who had won a **statue** in the **Olympics**. "**Mazel** tov," the mummy cried as he leaped in a **helicar** from **NASA**. It was hard to drive the helicar in the dark, but a **lighthouse** guided him along a **colossal road**.

That works just fine—but I want to give us a bigger challenge. I want us to learn not just the seven wonders but an interesting fact about each, plus when they were built and when they were destroyed. (At least, as far as historians know—a lot of these dates are estimates, and the Hanging Gardens of Babylon may never have existed at all. Plus, it can be hard to define "destroyed." Some of these wonders fell apart gradually over a thousand years. Fortunately, having read this book, you are now prepared to memorize this vague and possibly inaccurate information with total precision.)

9. Chapter 6: "Once Upon a Time: The Story Method."

TOTE & SHOE

Wonder	Date Built	Date Destroyed	Interesting Fact
Great Pyramid of Giza	2560 BC	NA	The oldest great wonder and the only one still surviving.
Hanging Gardens of Babylon	600 BC	AD 100	The only one of the seven wonders that nobody can prove was real.
Temple of Artemis at Ephesus	550 BC	AD 401	There were several versions of the temple. One was burned down by an arsonist who hoped the act would make everybody remember him. I'm not going to tell you what his name is because I think it's one of the few things that deserves to be forgotten.
Statue of Zeus at Olympia	430 BC	AD 475	Caretakers regularly poured olive oil on the statue to help protect the ivory in it.
Mausoleum at Halicarnassus	350 BC	1404	The tomb of King Mausolus, it made such an impression on the world that "mausoleum" now means any impressive tomb.
Lighthouse of Alexandria	300 BC	1480	There was a spiral ramp inside the lighthouse, used by pack animals bringing up wood for the fire at the top.
Colossus of Rhodes	280 BC	226 BC	Roughly the same height as the Statue of Liberty.

TOTE & KEY

117

To start, take a look at your list of memory palaces[10] in your memory notebook.[11] For the seven wonders, you need only seven distinct locations. But at the end of this book, you'll find a bunch of other things you might want to memorize, including the Seven Wonders of the Modern World and the Seven Summits of the Medieval World. If you'll want to memorize more wonders down the road, you may want to reserve a bigger palace.

Personally, I'm going to use my in-laws' house. It's a big suburban home, with a number of large, distinct areas that I can fill in with other lists. Plus, my wife and I already have a bunch of old papers stored in her parents' basement. I'm sure they won't mind if I throw in a handful of massive stone monuments as well.[12]

I'll start my memory walk at the washing machine. I could just plonk the Great Pyramid next to it—but that wouldn't be a very memorable image. Instead, I'll stick the pyramid *inside* the washing machine. I'll hear the swishing as the drum agitates it, and the screeching as the ancient stone scrapes against metal. I'll feel the rumble as the severely overloaded machine rocks back and forth. I'll smell that distinctive wet mummy smell emanating from inside. The more senses I engage, the more likely the image is to stick inside my head.

Now I need to add the date it was built. I could use number rhymes and picture a shoe, a hive, a stick, and Emperor Nero,[13] but since I've already done the work of learning a century PAO,[14] I'll picture my friend Neil with a delicious wedge of cheese. He's sitting inside the washing machine, and he doesn't seem to mind that he takes a mouthful of soap with every bite.

You'll notice I didn't need a mnemonic to remind me of our interesting fact about the Great Pyramid. That's because I've actually been there, so "still standing" is already chunked with "Great Pyramid" in my brain.[15]

10. Chapter 4: "There's a House in My Brain: Building Your Own Memory Palace"
11. Interlude: "Your Memory Notebook"
12. Chapter 2: "Dogs in Pink Tutus: Creating Memorable Images"
13. Chapter 8: "Bun, Shoe, Tree, Door: An Introduction to Remembering Numbers"
14. Chapter 12: "The International Number Mafia: Remembering Longer Numbers"
15. Chapter 1: "Memorizing Things You Already Know"

And because it's still standing, I don't need a date of destruction. My image is nearly complete—but I need one more detail. Some of the dates I'll be remembering are BC, and others are AD. So I'll use a standard modification.[16] Dates in BC are older, so they'll be covered in cobwebs. Dates in AD are newer, so they'll be sealed in shiny plastic wrap.

All in all, here's the first step on my memory walk:

Great Pyramid of Giza	2560 BC	NA	The oldest great wonder and the only one still surviving.

Instead of talking you through the rest of my images, I'm going to show them to you.

16. Chapter 3: "Miss-a-Sippy-Cup: Remembering Abstract Things"

TOTE & POO

goose + sew + cobwebs = 600 BC

Otis + sew + plastic = AD 100

hanging gardens

Hanging Gardens of Babylon	600 BC	AD 100	The only one of the seven wonders that nobody can prove was real.

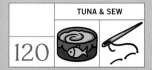

TUNA & SEW

120

Temple of Artemis at Ephesus	550 BC	AD 401	There were several versions of the temple. One was burned down by an arsonist who hoped the act would make everybody remember him. I'm not going to tell you what his name is because I think it's one of the few things that deserves to be forgotten.

TUNA & TEA

121

statue of Zeus

pouring olive oil

orc + lie + plastic = AD 475

ram + sew + cobwebs = 430 BC

Statue of Zeus at Olympia	430 BC	AD 475	Caretakers regularly poured olive oil on the statue to help protect the ivory in it.

TUNA & HONEY

Mausoleum at . . .

HelicopterNASSUS

mare + sew + cobwebs = 350 BC

Dictionary definition
of "mausoleum"

deer + sew + arrow + plastic = 1404

Mausoleum at Halicarnassus	350 BC	1404	The tomb of King Mausolus, it made such an impression on the world that "mausoleum" now means any impressive tomb.

lighthouse

deer + vase + plastic = 1480

spiral ramp

mouse + sew + cobwebs = 300 BC

Lighthouse of Alexandria	300 BC	1480	There was a spiral ramp inside the lighthouse, used by pack animals bringing up wood for the fire at the top.

TUNA & EAR

navy + sew + cobwebs = 280 BC

nun + egg + cobwebs = 226 BC

Colossus of Rhodes	280 BC	226 BC	Roughly the same height as the Statue of Liberty.

Now that I've stored that in my mind, I've got a new challenge: I've got to keep it there. So while you're generating your own memory walk, I'm going to put all that info into my flash card system.[17] Tomorrow, and a week from now, and months from now, I'll test myself on it; years from now, I'll still remember it.

You will, too. And more important, you'll know how to remember *anything*. What will you do with your new superpowers?

17. Chapter 10: "The Fickle Hippo of Memory: Retaining Memories for the Long Term"

TUNA & EEL

Appendix A: Leitner Box

If you've got access to a smartphone or a computer, it's easiest to use virtual flash cards. But if you don't (or if you just prefer the real, tree-based thing), here's how you can make your own Leitner Box.[18]

First, get the following:

- Blank index cards
- A box big enough to hold them
- Seven divider cards with tabs that stick up higher than the index cards
- A paper clip

On each of the divider cards, write a number from 1 to 7. Put them in your box in order.

Copy the schedule guide on page 79, and tape it to your box.

Write down the things you want to learn on your index cards, and put them all in section 1.

How Many Cards?

You can add as many cards as you want, but I would start with five to ten, then add more every day. After all, five cards a day is 1,825 cards by the end of the year. Adding them in gradually means you'll be reviewing them gradually. Dump them in all at once, and you'll have some days with nothing to review and some days when you're reviewing everything.

Put the paper clip on Day 1 of the schedule guide.

Every day, you'll perform the following steps:

- Look at the schedule for today to see which sections you're supposed to review.
- Test yourself on each card in those sections.
- If you get a card right, move it up one section. For example, if you get a section 3 card right, move it up to section 4.
- If you get a card wrong, drop it down to section 1.

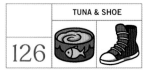

TUNA & SHOE

126

18. Named after its inventor, Sebastian Leitner.

- Once you've reviewed all the old cards, add any new cards to section 1.
- Review each card in section 1, and put it in section 2 once you know it.
- End your session by moving the paper clip to the next day.

That's it! As cards move to higher and higher sections, you'll review them less and less frequently. Once they leave section 7, you can dump them in a separate shoe box. In theory, you'll know every card in that shoe box permanently. (In practice, you might want to pull a handful of cards out of it a few times a year, just to make sure they haven't faded from your mind.)

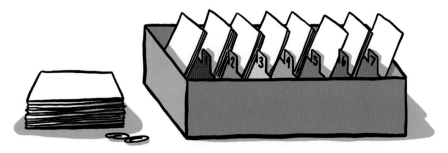

Appendix B: PAO in Chart Form

Here's a sample list of people, actions, and objects for the numbers 0 to 99. (Or, to put it in fancy mnemonist terms, here's my century PAO.) Feel free to use any of these images—but remember the Second Rule of Memory: *Everybody's brain is different.* If any of these don't work for you, make your own! I find it helps to stick to the Major System, but you don't have to. If the number 4 makes you think of your best friend, Susan, because you met her on your fourth birthday, who cares that there's no *r* in her name? As long as you know what number she stands for, that's what matters.

However you generate it, make sure you write down your entire list in your memory notebook. The mere act of doing so will set you on the road to memorizing it. Plus, if you have it all in one place, you'll be better able to spot potential interference. If your mom's name is "Angie," don't use "mom" for 33 and "Angie" for 26.

TUNA & KEY

127

Number	Letters	Person	Action	Object
0	Z, S	Sue (Storm, the Invisible Woman)	sew	saw
1	T, D	ET	tie	tea, dough, toe
2	N	Ann, Annie	knee, know	honey
3	M	Emma	mow, moo	Emmy Award, emu
4	R	Ray, Ra	row	ear, arrow, Oreo
5	L	(Princess) Leia, eel	lie, oil	lei
6	G, SH, CH, J	Ash (from Pokémon), Guy (Fawkes)	shoe (like shoeing a horse)	egg
7	K	(Doc) Ock	key, ache	oak
8	F, V	Eve, Ivy (Poison Ivy from *Batman*)	vow	ivy
9	P, B	ape, (Edgar Allan) Poe	pee	pie, poo
10	(T, D) + (S, Z)	Dizzy (Gillespie), Des, Desi, Otis	daze, taze	dice
11	(T, D) + (T, D)	Teddy (Roosevelt or bear)	tattoo, tote, toot	date, teddy
12	(T, D) + N	Tony (Stark), tuna, Dan, Odin	tune, attain, tone	tin, tine
13	(T, D) + M	Tom, Dom, (Dr.) Doom	time	ATM, atom, dime, team, dome
14	(T, D) + R	Terry, Dara, deer	tear	tire
15	(T, D) + L	Adele, Talia, doll	dial, deal	towel, tail
16	(T, D) + (G, J, CH, SH)	DJ, Diego, Dacia, Tisha	dig	tag
17	(T, D) + K	tick, Dick (Tracy)	take, tack	deck, dock
18	(T, D) + F	Daffy Duck, thief	dive, thieve	tofu, taffy
19	(T, D) + (B, P)	Dobby, tabby (cat)	tape, tap	tube, tub, top
20	N + (S, Z)	Ness (the Loch Ness Monster or Elliott Ness), (your) niece	nose	noose
21	N + (T, D)	(your) aunt, Ned (Flanders), Nat	knot, knit	nut
22	N + N	nun, Nina, nanny	nanny, naenae	onion
23	N + M	Nemo (from *Finding Nemo*), gnome	name	anime
24	N + R	(Emperor) Nero, Nora, weiner (dog)	honor	weiner

TUNA & IVY

128

Number	Letters	Person	Action	Object
25	N + L	Neal, Nel	nail	Nile, nail
26	N + (G, J, SH)	Angie, Inga	nag, noogie	nacho, inch, nosh, nog
27	N + K	Nick, Hank, hunk	honk, nuke, unhook	ankh, nook
28	N + F	Navy (officer), (your) nephew, Na'vi (from *Avatar*)	envy	navy, knife, nova
29	N + (P, B)	newbie	nap	nape, newbie
30	M + (S, Z)	moose, mouse	amaze	maze, hummus
31	M + (T, D)	Matt, Mitt	mute	mat, mate, moat
32	M + N	Minnie (Mouse), Mannie	moan	money, mine
33	M + M	(your) mom	mime	memo, meme
34	M + R	Mary (Queen of Scots), Omar, mare	marry	hammer
35	M + L	Milly, Molly, mule	mail	mule, mall
36	M + (G, J, SH)	Maggie, Meg, magi	mug	match
37	M + K	Mickey (Mouse)	make	mic, hammock, mocha
38	M + F	mafia	move	Humvee, movie
39	M + (P, B)	Moby (Dick), mob (of people)	mop, mope	map
40	R + (S, Z)	Rosie, Rose, Arisa	race, rise	rice, rose
41	R + (T, D)	Art, Rita, rat	rate, ride	art
42	R + N	Aron, Ron, Ariana, Iron (Man)	ruin, run	iron, rune
43	R + M	Romeo, ram	ram, roam	arm, Rome, army
44	R + R	warrior, rower	rear, roar	orrery, horror, error
45	R + L	Harley (Quinn)	rile, roll, whirl	rail, roll
46	R + (G, J, SH)	Rogue (from the X-Men)	rage	rag
47	R + K	(The) Rock, orc	rake	rack, rake
48	R + F	Robert (Frost or Louis Stevenson)	riff	ruff, reef, roof
49	R + (P, B)	Robo(cop), rabbi	rope, rap	rib, Europe, rope

TUNA & POO

129

Number	Letters	Person	Action	Object
50	L + (S, Z)	Elsa (from *Frozen*), Lois (Lane), Louis, Louise	laze, lose	lice
51	L + (T, D)	Lady (Lady Gaga or Lady from *Lady and the Tramp*)	light	lute, latte
52	L + N	Lenny, Leon, Leona, alien, lion	align, loan	line
53	L + M	lamb, llama	loom	elm, helium, lime
54	L + R	Laura, Larry	lower, lure	lure, lyre
55	L + L	LL (Cool J), Lily, Lola, Lulu, Lilah, Hillel, Layla	lol	lily
56	L + (G, J, SH)	Lego(las), Lego (minifigure)	luge	Lego, log
57	L + K	Luke (Skywalker), elk	lick	lake, lock
58	L + F	elf, Alf	laugh, live, love	loofah
59	L + (P, B)	(Idris) Elba, (Dua) Lipa	lap, leap	elbow, lap, loop
60	(G, J, SH) + (S, Z)	Josie, José, guys	choose	chaise, cheese
61	(G, J, SH) + (T, D)	Jed, Jedi, cheetah, goat	get, gut	agate, gat, gate
62	(G, J, SH) + R	genie, Ginny (Weasley), goon	chain, gain	China
63	(G, J, SH) + M	Jimi (Hendrix), Jamie, Jimmy	jam	gem, gum
64	(G, J, SH) + R	Jerry (from *Tom and Jerry*), (Edward) Gorey, ogre	jeer	gear
65	(G, J, SH) + L	Gail, ghoul, goalie	jail	Jell-O
66	(G, J, SH)+(G, SH)	judge	gag	jug, choo-choo
67	(G, J, SH) + K	Jack (Sparrow), geek, gecko	shake	shack
68	(G, J, SH) + F	Goofy, chef	shave	chive
69	(G, J, SH) + (P, B)	Gabby, Gabe	chop, gape	goop, Jeep
70	K + (S, Z)	cuz (your cousin), KISS (the band), Cassie	kiss	Hershey's kiss, kazoo
71	K + (T, D)	Kate (Middleton), Katy (Perry), cat	coat	coat
72	K + N	Conan (the Barbarian)	canoe, con	can, cane, cone
73	K + M	Kim	calm, comb	comb, camo
74	K + R	one of the cars from *Cars*	core, cry	acre, car

DIME & SEW

Number	Letters	Person	Action	Object
75	K + L	Kylie (Minogue), koala	coil, kill	coal, kale
76	K + (G, J, SH)	coach	cage	couch, keg
77	K + K	Cookie (Monster)	cook	cake, Coke, cookie
78	K + F	calf, Kofi (Annan), (a barista in a) café	cough	cave
79	K + (P, B)	okapi, Cap(tain America)	cope, cup. keep	cap, cape, coop
80	(F, V) + (S, Z)	Fozzie (Bear)	face, fuss	face, vase
81	(F, V) + (T, D)	photo(grapher)	fight, fit	fat, fate, foot
82	(F, V) + N	Finn (from *Star Wars*), Vin (Diesel), Vanna	fan, phone	fan, fun, phone, van, vein
83	(F, V) + M	F(reddie) M(ercury)	fume	fame, FM, foam
84	(F, V) + R	pharaoh, fairy	fear, fire, fry	ferry, fire, fur
85	(F, V) + L	Phil, foal	fail, file	vial, veil
86	(F, V) + (G, J, SH)	fish	vogue, voyage	fig, Fiji, fog, fudge
87	(F, V) + K	Vic, FKA (Twigs), Frida Kahlo	fake	FAQ
88	(F, V) + (F, V)	Viv	shouting Viva!	fife
89	(F, V) + (P, B)	Any vice president, FBI (agent)	fib	FBI (badge), fob
90	P, B + (S, Z)	Hobbes (from *Calvin and Hobbes*), Bozo (the Clown)	pace, pass	bus, peso, pizza
91	P, B + (T, D)	Pat, bat	pat	pita
92	P, B + N	bunny, Ben	open	bone, pan, penny, piano
93	P, B + M	(Hank) Pym, Pam, (Barack) Obama	beam (as in smile widely), bum	beam (as in wood), Pam (the spray)
94	P, B + R	Oprah, Barry, Aubrey	brew, pour, pray	berry, eyebrow, opera
95	P, B + L	Paul, Paula, Pele	blow, bully, pull	apple, pail
96	P, B + (G, J, SH)	(George) Bush	bash	bush, pig
97	P, B + K	Becky	back	book, pike
98	P, B + F, V	Buffy, Pav(lov)	behave, payoff, peeve	beehive
99	P + P	pope, puppy, Pepe, Pippa, baby	peep, pop	papaya, pipe

DIME & TEA

131

Appendix C: Common Names

50 common male names in the United States:

Aaron	Cameron	Hunter	Joshua	Nathan
Adam	Charles	Jackson	Juan	Nicholas
Aidan	Christian	Jacob	Justin	Noah
Alexander	Christopher	James	Kevin	Robert
Andrew	Daniel	Jason	Kyle	Ryan
Anthony	David	John	Logan	Samuel
Austin	Dylan	Jonathan	Mason	Thomas
Benjamin	Elijah	Jordan	Matthew	Tyler
Brandon	Ethan	José	Michael	William
Caleb	Gabriel	Joseph	Mohammed	Zachary

50 common female names in the United States:

Abigail	Ava	Hannah	Madeline	Rebecca
Addison	Brianna	Isabella	Madison	Samantha
Alexandra	Brittany	Jasmine	Maria	Sara
Alexis	Chloe	Jennifer	Megan	Savannah
Aliyah	Danielle	Jessica	Mia	Sofia
Allison	Elizabeth	Julia	Morgan	Stephanie
Alyssa	Ella	Katelyn	Natalie	Sydney
Amber	Emily	Katherine	Nicole	Taylor
Anna	Emma	Kayla	Olivia	Victoria
Ashley	Grace	Lauren	Rachel	Zoe

Appendix D: More Things to Memorize

The NATO Phonetic Alphabet

When you're spelling words, it's easy to mishear letters. Was that *s* or *f*? *P* or *b*? To prevent potentially life-threatening misunderstandings, NATO produced a list of the clearest example word for every letter. To spell "sip," you just say, "Sierra India Papa." Learn this list and never be misunderstood over the phone again.

Alpha	**J**uliet	**S**ierra
Bravo	**K**ilo	**T**ango
Charlie	**L**ima	**U**niform
Delta	**M**ike	**V**ictor
Echo	**N**ovember	**W**hiskey
Foxtrot	**O**scar	**X**-ray
Golf	**P**apa	**Y**ankee
Hotel	**Q**uebec	**Z**ulu
India	**R**omeo	

The Seven Summits

In 1986, Patrick Morrow became the first climber to reach the highest peak on every continent. Here are the mountains he summited, along with their heights.

Asia	Mt. Everest	29,035 feet
South America	Aconcagua	22,831 feet
North America	Denali	20,310 feet
Africa	Kilimanjaro	19,340 feet
Europe	Mt. Elbrus	18,510 feet
Antarctica	Vinson Massif	16,050 feet
Australia	Carstensz Pyramid	16,023 feet

The New Seven Wonders of the World

In 2007, over 100 million people voted to choose seven monuments that would make up a new Wonders of the World list. It was the largest poll in history. Here's what they chose.

Wonder	Location	Year Built
Great Wall of China	China	700 BC
Petra	Petra, Jordan	312 BC
Colosseum	Rome, Italy	AD 70
Chichén Itzá	Yucatán, Mexico	circa 6th century
Machu Picchu	Cuzco, Peru	circa AD 1450
Taj Mahal	Agra, India	AD 1632
Statue of Christ the Redeemer	Rio de Janeiro, Brazil	AD 1931

DIME & MOO

133

Morse Code

A ●▬	H ●●●●	O ▬▬▬	V ●●●▬
B ▬●●●	I ●●	P ●▬▬●	W ●▬▬
C ▬●▬●	J ●▬▬▬	Q ▬▬●▬	X ▬●●▬
D ▬●●	K ▬●▬	R ●▬●	Y ▬●▬▬
E ●	L ●▬●●	S ●●●	Z ▬▬●●
F ●●▬●	M ▬▬	T ▬	
G ▬▬●	N ▬●	U ●●▬	

I learned Morse Code with the help of this visual mnemonic:

A		H		O		V	
B		I		P		W	
C		J		Q		X	
D		K		R		Y	
E		L		S		Z	
F		M		T			
G		N		U			

DIME & EAR

Greek and Roman Gods

Greek God	Roman Equivalent	God of . . .
Aphrodite	Venus	Love and beauty
Apollo	Apollo	Music and art
Ares	Mars	War
Artemis	Diana	The hunt
Hestia	Vesta	Hearth and home
Hermes	Mercury	Travel and communication
Demeter	Ceres	Agriculture
Dionysus	Bacchus	Wine
Hades	Pluto	The underworld
Hephaestus	Vulcan	Fire and metalworking
Hera	Juno	Queen of the gods
Poseidon	Neptune	The sea
Zeus	Jupiter	King of the gods

The Dynasties of China

Xia Dynasty	ca. 2100–1600 BC
Shang Dynasty	ca. 1600–ca. 1050 BC
Zhou Dynasty	ca. 1046–256 BC
Qin Dynasty	221–206 BC
Han Dynasty	206 BC–AD 220
Six Dynasties Period	AD 220–589
Sui Dynasty	AD 581–618
Tang Dynasty	AD 618–906
Five Dynasties Period	AD 907–960
Song Dynasty	AD 960–1279
Yuan Dynasty	AD 1279–1368
Ming Dynasty	AD 1368–1644
Qing Dynasty	AD 1644–1911

DIME & EEL

135

Useful Conversions

Temperature in Celsius = (Temperature in Fahrenheit − 32) × $\frac{5}{9}$

Feet = meters × 3.2808

Inches = centimeters ÷ 2.54

Pints = 2 quarts = 20 fluid ounces

Relative Weight on Different Planets

Something that weighs one pound on Earth will weigh . . .

    0.38 pounds on Mercury

    0.91 pounds on Venus

    0.38 pounds on Mars

    2.36 pounds on Jupiter

    0.92 pounds on Saturn

    0.89 pounds on Uranus

    1.13 pounds on Neptune

Pi to 100 Digits

3.141592653589793238462643383279502884197169399375105820974944592307816406286208998628034825342117 0679

Things About Your Life

Some of the most relevant things you could memorize are things I can't include in this book! They might include:

- The birthdays of your friends and family members
- Your passport (or other ID) number
- Important phone numbers (even if they're already stored on your phone)
- The names of your elected officials
- Height of your hometown above sea level
- Latitude and longitude of your house

DIME & SHOE

136

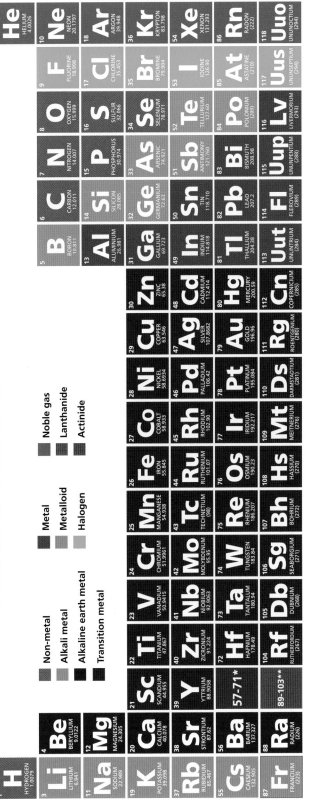

Periodic Table of the Elements

DIME & KEY

137

Bibliography

I deserve credit for very few of the ideas in this book. Many of the techniques I describe have been around for millennia, while others are the inventions of more recent mnemonic masters. Below, I've listed all the techniques I was able to attribute to specific individuals.

In addition to the books listed below, I found *Your Memory: How It Works and How to Improve It*, by Kenneth Higby, to be a particularly well-researched and informative guide to memory techniques, and I referenced it frequently while writing this book.

Note that many of the sources below were written for a grown-up audience, and some of them may contain material that is not appropriate for all ages.

CHAPTER 2: Many sources say the human brain contains 100 billion neurons. I wasn't able to find a persuasive source for that estimate, though. I was more convinced by the detailed methodology of Suzana Herculano-Houzel, who ended up with 86 billion neurons.

Suzana Herculano-Houzel, *Frontiers in Human Neuroscience 2009*; 3:31. Retrieved online: *ncbi.nlm.nih.gov/pmc/articles/PMC2776484/*

CHAPTER 3: I encountered the idea of assigning verbs like "freeze" or "burn" to masculine and feminine nouns in *Fluent Forever*, by Gabriel Wyner. If you want to use memory techniques to learn a foreign language, I've found no better guide.

CHAPTER 4: Results of MRI scans on memory champions were reported in "Routes to Remembering: The Brains Behind Superior Memory," Eleanor A. Maguire, John M. Wilding, and Narinder Kapur (2003).

CHAPTER 5: I don't know who came up with singing the Chinese Dynasties to "Frère Jacques," but I first learned about it on the Asia for Educators website (afe.easia.columbia.edu/), which in turn credits it to "the teachers on the College Board AP-World History Listserv."

CHAPTER 7: I learned about Ed Cooke's technique of asking yourself questions about people's faces from an article he wrote: "The Importance

DIME & IVY

of Observation," by Ed Cooke. *The Guardian*, January 15, 2012. Retrieved online: *theguardian.com/lifeandstyle/2012/jan/15/pay-attention-people-faces.*

CHAPTER 9: Greg Heffley's pillow-against-the-door technique comes from *Diary of a Wimpy Kid: The Ugly Truth*, by Jeff Kinney.

The technique of miming an activity to help your prospective memory comes from "Sustaining Prospective Memory Functioning in Amnestic Mild Cognitive Impairment: A Lifespan Approach to the Critical Role of Encoding," *Neuropsychology* (2018); Vol 32, No. 6, 634–644. Retrieved online.

CHAPTER 10: For an excellent look at everything science knows about retaining information for the long-term, I recommend *Make It Stick: The Science of Successful Learning*, by Peter C. Brown, Henry L. Roediger III, and Mark A. McDaniel.

CHAPTER 12: The Major System has its roots in a technique developed by Pierre Hérigone in the seventeenth century and further refined in Gregor Feinaigle's *The New Art of Memory* (1813). It was modified by various authors over the years—notably by Aimé Paris in 1825. Tony Buzan named it "the Major System" and popularized it in several of his books on memory, including *Master Your Memory* (2006).

CHAPTER 15: The Dominic System is described in *You Can Have an Amazing Memory*, by Dominic O'Brien.

Ed Cooke's method of memorizing cards is detailed in *The Four-Hour Chef*, by Timothy Ferris.

APPENDIX C: This list is based on the Social Security Administration's list of most popular baby names from 1990 to 2018.

APPENDIX D: Morse Code: The visual mnemonic is based on one in *Handbook for Girl Guides*, by Lord Robert Baden-Powell.

Chinese Dynasties: *afe.easia.columbia.edu/timelines/china_timeline.htm*

DIME & POO

Acknowledgments

In addition to the millennia of memory masters who invented the techniques I've described, this book wouldn't be possible without the help of numerous people. My thanks to:

My parents, my brothers and sisters, my in-laws, and especially Lauren, Erin, and Joseph, for their love, their support, and their patience with my lousy prospective memory.

My agent, Joan Paquette, for believing in and championing my writing.

My editor, Daniel Nayeri, for pushing me to make this the best and most thorough book it could be.

Barbara Malley, for her wonderful illustrations.

Designer Carolyn Bahar, Art Director Timothy Hall, Creative Director Christina Quintero, Managing Editor Jennifer Healey, Production Editor Barbara Cho, and the entire team at Odd Dot, for adding so much sparkle and delight to the book you now hold in your hands.

The Picturebookies, my picture book critique group (who didn't actually work on this book, but I'm mentioning them here because picture books don't usually have acknowledgments).

Elaine Boxer, Brian Horiuchi, Laura Mucha, Eric Peng, Adam Price, Caryn Tomljanovich, Denise Meyer, Kristin L. Gray, Kristen Gustafson, Toby Wahl, Kateri Paul, Aileen Hawkins, Lisa Clemans-Cope, Clifford J. Green, Fiona Burgos, Michael Ringel, Mary Supley, Loreen Heneghan, Steven Chivers, Karlyn Heiner Crotty, Anna Crowley Redding, Lucinda Shih, Pat Zietlow Miller, Adrienne Rubin, Eliza Rowley, Mark Miller, Juliet Clare Bell, Love Zubiller, and James Weiss, for suggesting interesting things to memorize.

And last, but certainly not least, I'd like to thank . . . uh, what's-their-name . . . You know, that person I'm incredibly grateful to but I'm just blanking on their name? That one. (If I've left you off the list, please assume this refers to you.)

TIRE & SEW

140